Linda Bruns

WISDOM BEFORE ME

Rise With The Wise

FEATURING FIFTEEN NEW YORK CITY TIME SQUARE CELEBRATED AUTHORS

Lauren Billings Erin Feldman Liza Marie Garcia Barbara Glanz
Joan Hammer Janelle Harris Kim Keller Jennifer Lea
Yolanda McIntosh Debora Porath Mindy Scarlett
Judy Shoulak Sarah Shoulak Helen Vella

Publish@nowscpress.com
www.PublishWithNOW.com
@nowscpress

Ordering Information:

Quantity sales. Special discounts are available on quantity purchases by corporations, associations, and others. For details, contact the publisher at the address above.

Orders by U.S. trade bookstores and wholesalers. Please contact: NOW SC Press: Tel: (813) 970-8470 or visit www.PublishWithNOW.com

Printed in the United States of America

First Printing 2022

ISBN: 979-8-9870349-3-4

DEDICATION

I lovingly dedicate this book to my family, especially my mother (watching over me, I miss you, Mom!), and my father, Jay Quillen, who just turned 90 years old and is still an inspiration to everyone he meets, my older brother and sister, Jay and Cindy, who have always looked after my well-being, even after I was well into being an adult. I am so fortunate to come from a loving, giving family who has always cared for each other and acts out of love above anything else. I also have a bonus mother, my mother-in-law Barbara, who is one of my biggest cheer leaders and consumate sales lady. Her support is unrelenting and filled with love and dedication to God and family.

Further dedication goes to my closest friends, Michelle Trias, Misty McGregor, Isis Trujillo, Sintia DeAsis, Jane Toombs, and Linda Wolf. These friends have supported me, believed in me and loved me every step of the way. A woman could not ask for better friends. It is not every woman who has such a large group of close friends which unconditionally love each other and offer unwavering encouragement. I am fortunate. With these friends, the laughter never ends and neither does the commitment to friendship. Thank you, ladies. I am honored to call you friend.

To my son, James Arthur Bruns, II (J.B.) who inspires me, teaches me, and loves me through it all. You are my greatest gift and I thank God for you every day. You continue to bring me joy and make me proud. From the day you were born until this present day, you continue to teach me how to be a better person. You are one special human being.

To my dear, amazing husband, Tim. You are my biggest cheerleader, you have stayed working side by side with me throughout this process and have been so patient. Even when, in the middle of this book project we started a new business, and your support has never wavered. I love you and could not have done this without you.

Finally, I want to thank all of the contributors for your transparency, dedication and commitment to make this a beautiful book of wisdom. The pages to follow will begin to unravel your stories to enlighten, inspire and empower women to persevere through their struggles. Women will understand they are not alone. Your wisdom is unmatched and a beautiful gift to the world. Thank you!

CONTENTS

INTRODUCTION
LINDA BRUNS

When we hear the word 'wisdom', we tend to think of the old, wise woman spewing tales. The truth though, is that we gain wisdom throughout our entire lives. Most of the time it is innate. We gain wisdom without realizing it. The collecting of wisdom is different for everyone, and some of us are more fortunate than others to not have to endure a great deal of pain and suffering to realize it. For others, there is much pain and many experiences of suffering brought on by various people and circumstances.

Wisdom guides us to our own successes. With our individual successes, we have the liberty to outline what success means to us when it might have nothing to do with a "keeping up with the Jones'" ideal or any other material type of success.

I believe when we fully understand where our wisdom comes from and how it contributes to our purpose, that is the beginning of a life of impact. Each and every person we meet provides us the opportunity to gain wisdom. As no one walks in anyone else's shoes, and as we have no idea what a person's perspective might be, learning of others' experiences can show us and teach us many life lessons.

There is no time like the present to start creating the life we want. As Abraham Lincoln once said, "The best way to predict the future is to create it." I believe we can make every day better than the last.

Wisdom is powerful. Wisdom is not always gained through pain, but it is often gained through love as well. For women, we often gain wisdom from our mothers, aunts, sisters, dear friends and even those friends who have betrayed us. No matter how your wisdom is gained, it must be cherished for the gift it becomes at different stages in your life. It should be cherished for its opportunity to help you grow and cherished for the impact it can make in your life.

The purpose of this book is to provide valuable and profound wisdom that will possibly impact your life and help you to turn a corner. The sharing of each woman's personal wisdom is just that - very personal. The sheer transparency of each story is captivating as they share their wisdom with you. I know this wisdom will help you and others create a purposeful path and unleash all the beauty you behold to live a more fulfilling life.

It warms my heart to know there are many women who understand the importance of providing support to each other and in embracing our differences and achieving all that life has to offer through sharing wisdom.

Buckle your seatbelt because we are going on a ride that will potentially change your life as you know it to a life filled with potential, fulfillment, and happiness. A life of wisdom gained, and wisdom shared. A life you can't wait to live each day. Today is the day!

DAMN RIGHT, THIS BIMBO WANTED TO FLY!

To my reader – The moment you think of giving up, think of the reason you started and why you've been holding on so long. Believe in yourself and don't ever give up on something you truly want.

I was born a perfectionist. Lucky me! This only set me up for future teaching moments throughout my life that have been eye-opening. I have learned along the way that being a perfectionist and expecting perfection is not necessarily the secret to success. Being a perfectionist can lead to feelings of not being "good enough" and can actually set us up for future failure.

I remember growing up, my mother would often remind me every day to do my homework. In my world, that was totally unnecessary. I was always self-motivated to get my homework done and strive for the "A". Yes, I was a perfectionist even in my earliest years.

Perfectionism does not leave much room for flexibility. When you expect perfection from yourself, you tend to expect the same from everyone and everything around you. Hello, reality. There

Perfectionism does not leave much room for flexibility.

are times when the gift of perfectionism comes in handy. But learning to loosen our grip on it allows us to be flexible, which may actually lead us to greater success. This was not a welcome lesson for me initially, but later, once I recognized it, it was one for which I am extremely thankful.

In school, I was in band, chorus, a little musical theatre and on the "Pom-Pom" Squad (schools now call it Dance Team). I started piano lessons at 6 years old, began playing oboe at 10, and sang whenever and wherever I could, including church. I have always been in love with music. One of my very earliest memories was singing in the church bathroom after the service—I must have been 4 or 5 years old—and this continued for some time. The acoustics were so great! I later learned from my mom that for all those years, all the adults meeting for their bible study could hear me through their back wall! They would just look at one another and, smile and there were some chuckles. At one point I found out people could hear me, but it didn't stop me.

I even used my love of singing to face my fear of walking down the stairs to my basement by myself. My mom told me if anyone was in our basement (which was my fear), they would simply hide if they heard someone coming. So I would sing as loud as I could with this *real weapon of defense*. I felt confident in my voice, having sung in choirs, like the Milwaukee Symphony Chorus, and performed in musicals as an adult, I've had the honor of being invited to sing the National Anthem many times over the years at large events. I believe having a musical talent is a gift from God and it's yet another gift to be good at something I really enjoy doing.

Growing up I would say for sure that I was a "girly girl", which is hilarious because according to my parents, I was "supposed" to be a boy. My parents had my sister first and based on the history of the family pattern, the next baby would be a boy. They had only a male name picked out. I was supposed to be Stephen. My dad didn't get his boy. He didn't get to enjoy *all* the father-son-type activities but we *did* hang out a lot—mostly when he was working in the garage and building things (like a fort for us and the neighborhood kids and an A-frame to lift the beds in our dorm room).

I remember being in the library as a ten-year-old and finding a book on careers. As I read through all the careers, I decided I wanted to deliver babies. This sounded like the best job, and I felt suited for it. Obstetrician… I could barely say it yet.

In college, I was pre-med with a psychology major. I worked like a dog each summer, taking on two or even three jobs to save up money for expenses throughout the school year. My goal was to be able to focus on school and not have to work while I was taking classes. During the spring of my sophomore year, I was donating blood, and nearly passed out there at the Student Union. They gave me the obligatory cookie and orange juice and I was fine—back to classes. A few hours later, I was on the verge of passing out again. It took me decades to learn it was the "Vasovagal Reflex" (reflex reduction blood pressure and heart rate). It only affects 10% of the population—lucky me. At that point, I realized being a doctor was not a good fit for me. It's not the blood that gets to me, it's the needles and unnatural cutting that does it. I thought, "I can still help people by being a Psychologist", so I continued in that direction.

Still pursuing my degree and also during my sophomore year, the Air National Guard piqued my interest. I was all for optimal ways to make money with anything interfering with my studies. The ANG required only one weekend per month and two weeks in the summer. I have to admit—I was not joining the military for some noble reason… but it fit into my plan to help me pay my bills. I enlisted for 6 years, which scared me a little. But I thought to myself, "Even if I *hate* it, it's only one weekend a month and two weeks in the summer, right?" First I had to get through Air Force Basic Training—and I chose a job with a short training school (Aerospace Control and Warning Systems Operator), so I could simply use my summer for training and be back in time for my junior year without missing a beat.

I'm not going to lie—Basic Training was not fun. After two weeks, we were allowed to call home. I wasn't able to reach my parents. After another week, I was able to reach someone—my dad. I remember crying as soon as he answered. He asked me if I wanted to come home. Through my tears I responded, "Noooo". Fortunately I was born with a determined and resilient personality. If I quit at that point, then three horrible weeks of my life would be wasted—with nothing to show for them. I believed in myself and knew I could and would make it through. I'm certain it was those qualities that got me through those tough times and exhausting training. I remained focused on my goal of having a job (with some benefits) that wouldn't interfere with school.

It didn't take long for me to realize that some in the Air Force didn't really want women in the military. There were bad attitudes, and obstacles and hindrances presented—you name it—that pointed to this fact. This was the 80s, when there were a lot fewer women stepping into these roles versus today.

One example of the not-so-female-friendly atmosphere at my home unit was when two of us had to sleep in a sleeping bag on the ground, in a tent in twenty-five-degree temperatures with seventeen other males because no one wanted to set up another tent. We were digging fox holes among many other back-breaking exercises right along with our unit and I never had an issue with all that was demanded of me. However, over and over again some would use whatever tactics they could to try to set us up for failure.

I wasn't going to let them get the best of me and I was developing a "thick skin" which has served me well in life.

If you weren't "one of the guys" you were discriminated against. This even went for some of the guys. If you weren't in the clique, in essence, no matter how good you were, you were set up to fail. I *was* good, so they had me training other airmen. I remember taking a "check ride" in the mobile radar van, tracking simulated aircraft on the radar screen. The exercise was to report and track everything I saw appear on the screen, with a maximum six to eight blips on the screen. However, this instructor was attempting to make me fail by adding more and more blips. At twelve, I finally failed. When the check ride was over, I held it together long enough to get to the bathroom and I cried. I was resolved to never let them *see* me cry, however. I wasn't going to give them the satisfaction. I told myself, "Never give up. Never give in. Never let 'em see you cry." And I would never quit, because if I quit—they win. I wasn't going to let them get the best of me and I was developing a "thick skin" which has served me well in life.

Not all squadrons are operated like the one I was in. It was just my bad fortune to be assigned there. But I know I am a better person because of the experience. The skills, the training, the struggles, all of it did make me a stronger, more well-rounded person. In a way, it shone a bright light on some of my weaknesses as a human being so I could smooth out the rough edges. It's like putting a diamond in the fire, the end result is a much more beautiful gem.

I lasted three years in that unit. It got to the point, though, on Wednesday before Guard Drill Weekend I would start to become nauseous, just thinking about reporting for duty on the weekend. By the time Saturday came along I was throwing up. The stress and anticipation of all that I was going to endure monthly was definitely getting to me. This anxiety went on for months.

Throughout my early years in the Guard, I would go along on the local flights after work just for fun, every few months. I just loved flying in the jump seat in the KC-135's and always asked a lot of questions. One evening on one of those flights, one of the pilots—who knew I was about to graduate from college—asked me if I had thought about becoming a pilot or a navigator. I said that I hadn't, and instantly thought, "How cool would that be?" I felt completely confident in the navigator position.

So I took the Air Force Officer Qualification Test (AFOQT) and began to undergo the medical evaluation. I visited the flying unit on base and was welcomed into the scheduling office, the heartbeat of the unit. There I met some of the pilots, navigators and boom operators and shared with them my interest in applying for a slot for training. I was later told that after I left, an old boom operator who was in the room at the time of my visit said, "That bimbo wants to fly!?" This is the type of attitude we have to deal with.

One Guard Drill Sunday morning, I went to speak with a Colonel at my unit to let him know I needed to run over to the medical clinic to have a test and I would be right back. He knew what I was trying to accomplish. He told me I wasn't going, saying, "Let me put it this way…if you go, don't bother coming back." Now, why would he take that stance? Why would he try to prevent me from going? I was not going to let anyone hold me back. I knew I could no longer remain in that squadron. I visited the recruiter on base and asked if he could find me a different unit, just until I (hopefully) got a pilot or navigator slot. He found me a Personnel position in the Security Police Squadron. These were great guys, many of whom were full time police officers in their communities. I was never so happy as when I left the first squadron.

I had chosen to pursue the Navigator position. The Pilot Board met first and the Director of Operations (D.O.) was heard to say, "That gal should have applied for a pilot slot—she would have gotten it" (referring to me). The main difference between pilot and nav is the vision requirement, pilots needing better vision than navs. I knew I had the brains and the perfect vision, but I wasn't sure I "had the hands". In some units, if you bust out of pilot training, you don't get to come back and apply for a nav slot. I went for the sure thing. Same pay, same rank and same trips. The only difference was it was easier for pilots to attain command positions and they may have the opportunity to one day go to the airlines.

When the day arrived for the Navigator Board, I was in a room with seven officers: Captains, Majors, Lieutenant Colonels and our Base Commander, a full bird Colonel. They were all sitting behind a boomerang-shaped table and there I was. A Staff Sergeant. They were shooting questions at me like a firing squad, my answer barely completed before the next question came. I *can* tell you that after interviewing with this Board, any and every other interview I had in my life seemed easy. The Base Commander asked me a rather tricky question—about the Commander of the first unit I was with. He asked me what I thought of him. Of course, my thoughts weren't positive, but it would be wrong to express it. I found positive, but truthful things to say about him. I later learned that they, too, had a negative view of him, but I know I did the right thing by not saying anything negative. It was important for me to be diplomatic and speak words that represented me well.

I recall receiving a rejection letter and immediately called the coordinator to let him know that while I was disappointed, I would be applying again—if that was alright with them. I was told I was a great candidate and I should definitely do so. They had to select the Navy

Flight Engineer out of the four candidates as they only got one nav slot per year and they needed to send someone who was a sure thing. He was very experienced and could already perform some aspects of the job. Several months later, I heard he was disqualified due to his vision. I called the coordinator to check in again, hoping they hadn't forgotten me. I was told he was so glad I called because I was their second choice! They lost their slot, but 6 months later they were able to get a "fall-out slot"; one that someone else loses for one reason or another. The lesson of persistence is one that has paid off many times in my life. Once I began training it went like this: Officer Training – 6 weeks; Undergraduate Navigator Training (UNT) in California – 9 months; Combat Survival Training and

I refused to allow him to deter me or let his attitude get in the way of achieving my goal.

Water Survival Training (the only part I feared) in Washington state – 3 weeks; Specialized Undergraduate Navigator Training (SUNT) in California – 3.5 months. I took leave from my full-time civilian job and was placed on active duty for a total of 16 months.

I was injured during Survival School and found out how really tough I was, continuing with an extremely painful medial meniscus tear in my left knee. They had told us if we quit at any point for any reason, we would have to start over again. Once again, I wasn't quitting, otherwise the time I put in thus far would have been wasted. I later reinjured the knee while stationed in Cairo for Desert Storm and never considered for a moment leaving to have it repaired. It was painful climbing the ladder into the aircraft, but it didn't prevent me from doing my job.

During UNT I had over 50 instructors, between classroom, aircraft and simulator and they were all pretty decent. I think it was our Celestial Navigation instructor who stood in front of our class and actually said, "I don't think women should be in the military." As shocking as it was, I chose to ignore his remark and take advantage of his knowledge, reminding myself to keep my eyes on the prize. I refused to allow him to deter me or let his attitude get in the way of achieving my goal. I knew that if I didn't believe I belonged there, why would anyone else?

We were subject to over 50 check rides—some in the simulator and some in an aircraft. I had a range of performance: Excellent, Good and Satisfactory…never failing a mission. In our class of 72 students (only 7 of which were women), I was "on course" to rank 4th or 5th in the class. We were on our very last check ride, in a simulator this time.

My preflight was unrushed and uneventful and we "took off". Everything was going great for this low-level mission. However, about 20 minutes in, some bizarre coordinates were showing in my Inertial Navigation System (INS). These were coordinates that didn't make any sense as they were ones from a different part of the world! I knew I needed to do something fast. I set my course to ensure I would stay in my corridor and I had the brilliant idea to shut down the equipment and bring it back up again, reinitializing the INS with coordinates matching what I figured my current position was. When your aircraft is going 7 miles a minute, a lot happens fast. I fully recovered but unfortunately, while I was reestablishing my position, I broke out of the corridor by a mile or two. I busted. My first—and only. There went any hope of being 4th or 5th in the class. But I was proud to earn my wings. It was years later that I put it together. I remembered who my instructor was for that final ride—the officer who made the stupid remark to our class about women in the military. I had been set up. Was I the highest ranked female?

I've learned over the years that being a woman often means having to be far better than our male counterparts in order to be considered "almost" as good as they are. It's all perception. This didn't motivate or demotivate me. It just frustrated me. I did and will always give my personal best to achieve my goals. The incredible wisdom I learned from my varied military experience is the art of never giving up.

Looking back, I know the traits that got me through challenging times were persistence, positivity, resiliency and belief in myself. I also learned from my time in the military was how important it is to remain flexible. This skill is very helpful in all relationships, including those with my husband and children. Flexibility has also helped create more success within the careers I had post-military, and also the businesses my husband and I have owned and operated. I am grateful for all those wisdom lessons I lived through and benefitted from, and at the end of the day…damn right this "bimbo" wanted to fly! And did it well!

*To Doug, thank you for your undying love,
unfailing support and enduring belief in me.*

*To Dalton and Landon, because of you, I've learned to be a
better person…and there's nothing wrong with being "extra".*

*To Linda, thank you for getting me to step out of my
comfort zone (once again), for recognizing that sharing
my story could truly help others and for inviting me to
join you on this incredible journey.*

Linda's Wisdom Wrap-Up

Never giving up is the key, no matter what! When you envision the end result, no amount of degradation or obstacles can waiver your stride.

YOLANDA MCINTOSH

CEO/FOUNDER
MIZMACMARKETING

FAITH IN LIFE'S TRIBULATIONS- NO ONE SAW THE GUN

Remember God is still in the blessing business and He is still performing miracles in people lives. God is waiting for you to call on His name so you can become transformed, healed, delivered, and set free!

O ne of my earliest memories is as a seven-year-old hiding behind the couch when a drunken brawl broke out at a family gathering. For some reason, unknown to me at the time, my Great Aunt Juanita disliked my twin cousins Birdie and Abbie. Abbie had done something that my aunt took offense at, and she had my young cousin in a chokehold and his face was red as a beet. Birdie was trying to break my aunt's hold on her brother, and soon the entire family was shouting and jostling for position.

I was scared. I was crying and the only thing I could think to do was hide behind the couch. From my vantage point, I saw Birdie go upstairs. The noise kept getting louder and louder as everyone got in the fight. I heard Birdie coming down the stairs in the hall, and I knew this was going to be trouble. Frightened and confused, I needed my

No one saw the black .22 gun in her hand but me.

mother to hold me, but everyone's focus was on the violence in the middle of the room. Birdie fought through the crowd, and no one saw the black .22 gun in her hand but me.

Birdie faced my aunt and pointed the gun at her, demanding that she let her brother go. The pushing and screaming got louder. Birdie's eyes looked soulless and unrecognizable. My aunt dared her to shoot and she refused to release her brother. She even smiled at Birdie and called her a "White H….". Birdie pulled the trigger. Aunt Juanita began to scream and she let go of Abbie. My great grandmother screamed, "What did you do?"

No one heard my cry or screams. I was abandoned and hiding behind a couch for safety. I stayed there for hours. I listened to my cousin tell Abbie to leave the house because the cops would be coming. Everyone was clearing out. Birdie removed the shell of the .22 bullet from the dining room wall. She covered the gun with a red cloth that I think was a t-shirt, buried it in the backyard, then plastered and painted the hole that was in the wall.

Aunt Juanita died as a result of the gunshot and prior medical problems. The authorities never knew Birdie was the one who shot her. My mother left town for New Jersey, and I was alone with my great grandmother. Birdie continued to dominate my life as she became one of the biggest drug dealers in our town. She used me as a "mule", hiding drugs in my jacket as she and I would play in the park. I did not know what was going on, of course, and at no time did anyone tell my mother in New Jersey.

Now as an adult, I now know the intense effect this type of early trauma can have. I had to live through many more scenes like the one, and there were other times I wondered if I would still be alive when morning came. Fortunately for me, after time I learned to hand things over to God, and to not hold grudges or use past trauma as an excuse not to 'do good."

With all I survived as a child, I felt called into ministry at an early age. I worked every part of the ministry, including being the chorus teacher, Bible study teacher, and being part of the missionary department. Additionally, I was an usher, evangelist, secretary, and even learned how to preach. Finally, I received my license to become an ordained Pastor.

I helped build and began my mother's church supporting "True Love Full Gospel Ministries." I was the first church to be birthed from there called "New Beginning Ministries International". Our church body is a healing and deliverance ministry.

Looking back, I now understand why I had to experience all of the suffering, abandonment, a broken family, and even a dysfunctional marriage. It was so I would learn firsthand about healing, the laying of hands, as well as binding and building a strong prayer life with God. I had to learn how to trust the Holy Spirit and to be led by the Holy Spirit. Although it is often tough, we must learn to trust God's process, and know that all is done in God's timing. He's the one with the master plan and you need to trust His process.

Another piece of wisdom that I have acquired along the way is to listen when opportunity knocks. A prophet of God who prophesied over my life said I would be a brand name. At the time, I was still married, and my married name was Grubb. However, my maiden name was McIntosh. His comments started to make sense. I decided to start a business called Miz Mac Marketing LLC and this opened the door for me to work with some really amazing people.

The next piece of wisdom I would like to share is the importance of faith. My last pregnancy was a very difficult one. At three months along, I began to have pains and when it seemed that my water had broken. I cried out to God, pleading not to lose the baby. I called my husband, Ron, pleading with him to come home immediately because I thought I was losing the baby. I cried and was afraid to get up from the bed. Ron got me to the doctor, who immediately ordered an ultrasound.

In the examination room it got very quiet as my doctor kept circling around my stomach without saying anything, and we began to get really worried. At last, the doctor looked up and said, "It's a miracle! I do not know how else to describe it! We were wrong with our first scan. You actually had twins, and you lost one, but one is still in there." Then he showed us our son's strong heartbeat!

Although it was a miracle that one of my twins survived, the next few months were very difficult. I was placed on complete bed rest as there was a chance without surgery I could lose the other twin. I agreed to the necessary operation and the result was successful. However,

I had to be on a breathing apparatus, as I was not breathing on my own. The breathing tube made me choke, but I kept praying and had faith that I'd breathe on my own again. At long last, I did!

After this all happened, I continued to pray, and I was placed in a room with a very nice woman. As I fell asleep, to my astonishment, I woke up to a man's voice, and it was my roommate's father, asking her why she was in there with a N- person. Never in my life had I ever thought I would be attacked on that level. His daughter asked her mom why she didn't leave him at home. My roommate pleaded with him to keep his voice down so he did not wake me up. I pretended to be asleep.

Having just got out of surgery, I was paralyzed from the waist down. I felt like the devil was attacking me from all different levels. Instead of resting, I couldn't help but listen to that mess. My whole family, including my stepmother, cousins, and my great grandfather were mixed race people. I never thought that I would ever have to face this type of hate. I asked the nurse to move me out of the room. The nurse came and kicked the mother and father out and my roommate apologized as I was leaving.

I truly believe we can call upon our angels to assist us with our day-to-day life.

We must remember we do not wrestle flesh and blood but with principalities and darkness. We are being tested. The bible says rebuke the devil and he shall flee. I continued to pray and begged God to save and heal my baby's life, and I was released a few days later.

At month seven, I had to be admitted to the hospital yet again. I was beginning to feel like the Rahway Hospital was my second home. The doctor did not want me to go into early labor, so they gave me medication to stop the contractions. I did not respond positively to this medication and began to feel like I was having a heart attack. They stopped the medication as the doctor said, "Yolanda, we need you to relax. Your blood pressure is up." They were additionally concerned that my sight was being affected, as I was also having trouble seeing clearly.

My husband Ron was terrified for me, but I had an incredible peace within because I knew God was present and I knew my angels were standing guard to watch over me. I have always believed that

Michael and Raphael are my angels of protection. When I was a kid, I drew them on an ink painting with pastel chalk and I truly believe we can call upon our angels to assist us with our day-to-day life.

As my son was finally born, and he was so pale that it looked like he was not getting enough oxygen. I had lost so much blood that I was unable to move properly and had partial paralysis in my left leg. So, once more, I focused on prayer, particularly Psalm 91, as I know by memory. Through this prayer, I remember saying to God, "Why me?" and "Please fight on my behalf dear Lord."

The next morning, the doctor told me how pleased he was that I was awake and improving. He had been concerned about my blood loss and how it would affect my recovery. I told him that I was not worried as I had prayed before I closed my eyes. His response was, 'You serve a powerful God."

The hospital made the determination to release my baby, but they would not release me until I could at least walk across the room. I knew it was time to pray hard and have much faith. The prayer and the faith worked as I was released at the same time as my son and was able to take my baby home.

This is just some of my life's journey and I hope as you read this, you know that no matter what life throws at you, there is a life experience for every occasion within the Bible. There might be stories in your life that parallel Daniel or Job. Each and every story in the Bible is a life experience that has a message for you, which can help you learn what you need to learn from God.

I leave you with these words of wisdom: Look to see and reevaluate what is happening in your life. Look at it from many different angles, but look at things spiritually first, because in that view, you will find clarity. If you look at yourself with spiritual eyes and allow the Holy Spirit to convict and guide you, you will hear His voice. You just need to stop and listen as He talks to us all the time. The Holy Spirit is with us each and every day, but it's up to you to listen to that one quiet voice.

To my family and friends, it is an honor to be a part of this book, as I get the chance to share some of my life story with you all.

Linda's Wisdom Wrap-Up

When you lean on your faith, it provides clarity in your trust in God.

JUDY SHOULAK

CEO
RELATIVELY SPEAKING

GRIT WILL CREATE A HAPPY LIFE

I am dedicating this chapter to my lovely daughter, Sarah, who inspired me to be a part of this anthology. Sarah has worked so hard to become her best self and create her own path. I don't think she realizes how many others she has inspired along the way.

I grew up in a small town in Wisconsin, and as a child, I didn't have a family support system that most people would consider "normal." My mom passed away when I was ten, and I had to make my own way and pay my own way from a very young age. With her taking her own life, there were a lot of complicated feelings that accompanied my mom's death. As a matter of fact, I think we all just said she had a heart attack for many years…perhaps out of shame, guilt, or just not wanting to acknowledge it.

Within a year of my mom's death, my dad got remarried to someone who would prove to be a very challenging stepmother. There were some tumultuous years between the ages of ten and fifteen, which prompted me to move in with my sister, Sharon, and her husband; for that, I am forever grateful.

I am also very grateful that although my parents were not capable of providing the typical structured family life, I know they did their best. I always felt very much loved by both my mom and dad and I knew they were always proud of me.

The fact that my early life wasn't easy for me fueled my determination to succeed.

No one in my family had ever gone to college, but I set the goal that I would earn a four-year degree. After high school, I worked full-time and attended a community college, where my goal was to achieve a 4.0 grade point average. I worked really hard, earned that 4.0, and was named valedictorian of my class. I was so proud of how far I had come. I was halfway to my goal, or so I thought, when I was devastated to find that many of the four-year colleges wouldn't accept my community college credits. It was a setback, but I was determined that I WOULD get my four-year degree, and I wasn't going to start over. I just needed to figure out how to make it happen.

While in high school, I started working part-time in retail for JCPenney. At the time, I just needed a part-time job to make some money while going to school. However, I found I loved customer service and working with people and eventually I saw that I could take a job and make it into a career. So, when I was twenty-one, I decided to pursue a management career at JCPenney. This was a huge step for me. Not only was I young, but it was an era where things were very different for women in the workplace. It also meant I had to move to a different city.

I was moving away from everything that was familiar to me. However, that step forward launched my career. I ended up working at JCPenney for nine years, gaining management experience in various operations positions. By the mid 80s, I decided I really wanted to work for a smaller company, so I took a position as a general manager for the Original Cookie Company, a small chain that would eventually be bought out by Mrs. Fields.

I still had my goal of earning a four-year degree, and a few years after joining the Original Cookie Company, I discovered that a private college in Milwaukee *would* accept my community college credits. So, while working full-time, I went back to school at a private university where I had to pay my own way. This should demonstrate my determination.

One of my assignments for a business class was to write a case study about the Original Cookie Company. In doing this research paper, I found that the company hired managers for their operations skills more than leadership skills. My recommendation was for the company to have a centralized training function, ongoing management training and development, and, of course, tuition reimbursement.

I was really proud of this paper, and I decided to do something bold. Sometimes opportunity comes to you, but I've learned that sometimes you must create your own. I decided to send my report to the president of the Original Cookie Company. And guess what? The company agreed with my findings. In fact, they offered me a job at the home office in Cleveland, where they wanted me to build the training program for the company's two hundred general managers.

I consider this my biggest career break ever. At the same time, it was also my biggest risk. By this time, I was married and had a one-year-old child. Moving to Cleveland would mean uprooting my family and moving to a city where we didn't know anyone. It wasn't just a step forward but a giant leap of faith.

This also gave me the confidence that I could accomplish absolutely anything I set my mind to.

Taking on this new job opened a whole new world for me. But the move also meant another setback in my quest to earn my bachelor's degree. You see, moving to Ohio meant I had to leave the university in Milwaukee, where I was only ONE credit shy of getting my degree. I could transfer to a school in Columbus, but in order to receive a degree from Capital University, I had to establish residency, which meant taking a minimum of thirty-six credits from their school. I had a new job, and, by this time, two young kids. However, I was determined to earn my degree. So, I spent a year working full time and taking a full load of classes.

AT LAST, in 1991, THIRTEEN years after I started working on my degree, I received my B.A. in Business Administration from Capital University in Columbus, Ohio. I consider this one of the most significant accomplishments in my life. This also gave me the confidence that I could accomplish absolutely anything I set my mind to.

In 1993, I joined OfficeMax as Director of Training. Two years later, I was promoted to Vice President of Human Resources, where I had the distinction of being the only female vice president in a group of forty VPs at OfficeMax. One of my jobs was to help diversify the company. Let me give you some perspective - at one point, all seventy of our regional managers were white males. Talk about being outside your comfort zone!

It was at OfficeMax, however, that I gained my next, most important piece of wisdom. I was working for one of the executive vice presidents, and I was working like a crazy woman. I had been given the feedback that I could be perceived as a bit defensive. He told me, "Judy, you don't have to be perfect." No one had EVER told me that before, and I was always striving so hard for perfection that I was always exhausted!

Somewhere along the way, I missed the memo on how to take care of myself.

And, when you are exhausted you tend to get defensive. So, I began to be kinder to myself and less bent on being perfect.

I joined Buffalo Wild Wings in 2001 as the Vice President of Human Resources. We had about 150 restaurants, and our growth was really starting to take off. On the day we became a public company in 2003, our Vice President of Operations resigned. Because of my background in operations, I was promoted to oversee company operations. That's really where my passion was, so it was a perfect opportunity for me. Franchise operations were added to my responsibilities after about a year and eventually I led all of the operations of Buffalo Wild Wings, taking on the role of President of the North America brand in my last three years with the organization.

From a personal and professional standpoint, I really thought I could do it all, be an amazing leader in a career that I loved with a company I felt completely in sync with. Be a fabulous mom to three children whom I loved so dearly and be a great wife to my dear husband, Jim, who had decided to stay home with our children, but reality spoke loud and clear. I really was not superwoman. Somewhere along the way, I missed the memo on how to take care of myself. Quite frankly, with my determination and focus, I was able to attain amazing professional and financial success, but it ended up being at the expense of my health.

For about twenty years, I lived on less than five hours sleep per night. In 2001, I was diagnosed with breast cancer. My life would never be the same after that. I had spent so much time in the business world looking at Type "A" personalities and Type "B" personalities, but now it was time to look at Type "C" personalities - cancer personalities - those who are always taking care of everyone else except themselves.

I did a major reassessment and reorganization of my life, and this was the result:

SLEEP: I am super focused on making sure I get ample sleep each night. I now regularly get between seven and eight hours of sleep each night.

EXERCISE: I am pretty obsessed about making sure I get 10K steps per day. This is something I have been doing for years. I also try to make sure I get my strength exercises as well.

PRAYER: This has always been a focus for me, but even more so since breast cancer. This really helped me focus on my appreciation for the role God has played in my life and how grateful I am.

MEDITATION: This has been a huge part of my mindfulness in the past five years. I start 95% of my days with mediation. This really helps me take control of a mindful approach to managing my days.

FOOD/NUTRIENTS: I am extremely conscientious of making sure I manage my weight in the healthiest way possible. For years, I focused on my weight, but now I am more concerned with making sure I am doing it the right way!

I beat cancer and kept on working in a job I loved. However, in 2017, things began to change. We had an activist investor presenting many challenges to our methods of operations at Buffalo Wild Wings. A significant challenge was made to our core philosophy of owning a significant amount of our restaurants. Suffice it to say, for me, it was not worth the battle. It seemed like a sign to me that this was the time to make the move to begin the next chapter of my life.

I spent months on plane rides thinking of what my next chapter would be, and I spent much time thinking of what I really enjoyed, such as public speaking, inspiring others, and helping people who just need a little additional support.

Somehow, these thoughts led me to working with each of my three children in their areas of passion. My math-oriented son, Joe, was working at a local *Mathnasium*. It was almost right next door to my local *Buffalo Wild Wings*, and it just appeared so simple. It was just a few tables in a space teaching kiddos math. It was much less expensive than the space, expense, and energy of managing the forty TVs and all of the other equipment needed to run a *Buffalo Wild Wings*! He had asked if I would ever consider opening a *Mathnasium* - of course, I said yes. Once we asked the Franchisor if a Minneapolis territory was available, there was no turning back.

My son, Jake, was my musician guy. It only made sense that we would open some type of music school together. He did some investigation and brought forth the idea of opening a *"Bach to Rock"* *Music School*. We decided to take the leap. Fast forward five years, and we have signed an agreement to have five *"Bach to Rock"* *Music Schools* in the Minneapolis area. For these businesses with my two sons, we really felt that the franchise model would be the best. If we could become part of an organization that could show us a model for success, it would be in our best interest. Why try to reinvent the wheel if we could become part of a reputable brand that could show us the ropes? We are positive this was the right decision!

As for my daughter Sarah, we decided to go out on our own and start a business called *"Relatively Speaking."* After all, we are relatives, and we would be speaking together. We provide workshops customized to organizations (typically in the areas of building high-performing teams, creating culture, resolving conflict, and executing effectively).

Why try to reinvent the wheel if we could become part of a reputable brand that could show us the ropes?

We also are both vice presidents of the Gapology Institute, where we provide workshops on how to identify gaps in execution and then how to close them.

As I started working with all three of my children, I looked forward to working side-by-side with them, sharing my business experience while letting them be able to fulfill their dreams in their individual areas of passion. It was a bit harder than I expected to start up three businesses at the same time, and they obviously pulled me in many directions. I did not feel like I was at my best in any area, and all areas were new and would have been challenging in the best of circumstances. I often thought that my children, who have admired my success as a business leader, must have wondered, "Who is this crazy woman?"

There has been one common theme in all of our businesses. It is always about doing the right thing for the long-term success of the business according to the strategy we set and the commitments we agreed to as a family team. I have to say that my biggest revelation is really how the tables have turned and how much wisdom I have gained from my children. Once we learned how to effectively work together, we have become great teammates. With ever-changing technology, I appreciate their guidance, and they have "fresh eyes" to see new ideas for all our businesses.

I am most grateful that I learned to work hard and take responsibility for my actions. I have definitely made some mistakes in my life, but I have learned from them and I don't often repeat the same mistakes. I look at my life like a game of bowling with bumpers in the gutters that keep bouncing me back. I may not get all strikes, but I have combined my strikes with enough spares that have enabled me to have a wonderful life.

It is quite joyous to help be the "bumper" in the lives of many others, and for this, I am so grateful. The wisdom I would like you to take away from my story is that you don't have to be perfect. Just always try your best, while at the same time, making it a priority to look after yourself.

I am dedicating this chapter to all the women who might have thought the path to success is easy. We all have obstacles; we must be positive, work hard and seek/accept help from others!

Linda's Wisdom Wrap-Up

Reaching heights of success doesn't always mean your life is in balance.

JENNIFER LEA

FOUNDER & CEO
ENTRY ENVY

PLAY YOUR CARDS

For the reader, I hope you have the fearlessness
to pursue your dreams and choose happiness.

I have two daughters, Lexie and Lauryn, who are eleven and thirteen. As I sat down to write this, I thought of them first and foremost. What am I trying to teach my daughters as I raise them? What do I wish I would have done differently? If I died today, what would I want them to remember?

1. Don't judge a book by its cover. Be nice to everyone and build relationships…it's a really, really small world.

2. Opportunities to shine exist everywhere, and life is all about what you make of it. Play the cards you're dealt to the very best of your ability.

3. Get up, dress up, show up, and do your part. No matter what.

As children of recently divorced parents and the tween years, I would venture to say that Lexie and Lauryn may be in one of the most difficult stages of life. Every chapter of life has a different story. The middle school and high school years were certainly challenging for me. It wasn't that the academics that were challenging, it was my gift of leadership that was labeled as "bossy" by my peers. I hated "teamwork" until I was in management and learned I got to design and decide who was on the team as opposed to a teacher. Game changer.

I boil the successes in my life down to the *Golden Rule* that my parents drilled into my head: *Be nice to everyone…it's a really, really small world.*

I'm sure I wasn't as nice to everyone in junior high and high school as I could or should have been. It's one of my regrets. I didn't appreciate how small the world really was until I graduated from college. This became crystal clear when I applied for a position and the hiring director knew my mom. Or when my very first employee's uncle happened to be my dad's good friend. Or when I realized I served drinks at my side job to my future employer at a law firm. The list can go on and on, when time after time, I was so grateful for the connections I had, and that my entire family subscribed to the golden rule. This single point has opened more doors for me than any amount of education ever will.

It took me all of two seconds to realize I was going to look for a new job!

Before we go too much further, let me explain where I've been, how I got to where I am today, and where I'm going, to give you the context of the words of wisdom I would like to share.

It was December of 1999, when I graduated from college with a business degree with a major in marketing a semester early. I had secured employment six months before graduation at a bank where I had been working at nearly full time and I reported directly to the CEO in charge of a project to open a new branch out of state. On my first official day on the job, January 4, 2000, I showed up in my new power suit and was greeted by someone I had never met whom uncomfortably explained that the CEO had been let go by the board of directors on December 31st. He said my position had been eliminated and asked would I like to be a bank teller instead. It took me all of two seconds to realize I was going to be looking for a new job.

The next position I applied for, and landed, was the marketing director for a plastic surgery practice. The most important things I learned from that position were the power of customer service and "do whatever it takes" to get the job done right. I worked no less than 70 to 80 hours a week and found I loved handling a ton of different projects in a fast-paced, demanding environment. In a nutshell, I prefer running around like a chicken with my head chopped off doing about 50 different things all day long. Turns out, I am very good at this! I played the hand I was dealt and made the most of my position for nearly six years. I learned as much as I possibly could and built long-standing relationships that have served me time and time again.

In my next role, I found myself as the youngest law firm administrator in the country. I had lost the battle with five litigation attorneys that comprised the firm's executive committee telling them I was not qualified to run their firm as I recommended them to hire me for the position in which I had originally applied, their marketing director. I had no idea what I was doing managing a law firm, but if I was going to "fake it until I made it" it became very clear that I was going to have to quit my second job as a cocktail waitress and figure it out fast. Once again, I worked 70 to 80-hour work weeks and made the most of every opportunity. The firm had 26 lawyers and as many staff. During the next nine years, I learned a tremendous amount about business, operations, marketing, billable hours, employee benefits, and most of all, how to work with egos and difficult personalities. My written and verbal communication skills improved by leaps and bounds. I developed thicker skin than an elephant, learning to take nothing personally.

I developed a thicker skin than an elephant, learning to take nothing personally.

In 2013, my friend who worked at another law firm in Omaha was relocating to Maine. I was sought out by the firm to replace her. Once again, I expressed concern to the firm's board of directors, sharing that with my two children (one-year-old & three-year-old), and while halfway through earning my MBA, I was not the right candidate for this new position. Additionally, I explained the timing was wrong as once I graduated, I intended to become a law firm consultant. My exact words during my interview were, "I wouldn't even hire me right now." And yet, they assured me they had a "family friendly culture" and I joined them as their new executive director. They weren't kidding in the least bit. Not all law firms are not created equal. Their culture was a welcome change, and I would make my home there for nearly the next eight years.

In my first year there, I was three-quarters of the way through a $50,000 degree and authoring a book that I started writing to kickstart my future new consulting business. Through the process of writing a book about how to manage a law firm, I realized that I didn't want to build that business; I didn't want to argue with lawyers the rest of my life about how to do things different; I didn't want my only purpose in life to help law firms be more profitable. This realization was monumental and heartbreaking.

I went back to the drawing board to look at my future. Literally, I created a vision board, something I had never done. Starting with a bunch of magazines I literally cut out with scissors what I was drawn to and visions of what I thought my future might hold. I started with a five-year vision board, asking myself what I thought five years from now would look like? Time with friends and family, volunteer time, a huge pantry, a Lexus, vacation time, and a lake house.

In the business world, we are very intentional about our professional goals and company objectives. We do annual strategic planning. We do our annual budgets, focusing each month on our financials. We revisit our project and team goals every quarter. However, how often do we stop to do this in our personal life? If we don't, life will still happen. Life will just pass by. With or without deliberate decisions for our lives, life moves forward on its own.

Here I was in this truly "oh shit" moment. I had no idea what I wanted to do with the rest of my life, but what I did know was that I had an expensive education, two children, and a challenging marriage. I decided to put it all on the shelf for the time being. I had a job I actually loved, two girls to raise, and would try to make the best of my marriage. I am the type of person who can and does fix everything, so with all certainty, I could fix this, too. But I couldn't. I filed for divorce in January 2020. Little did I know the COVID pandemic would hit two months later and rock my world even harder. It was a true blessing to shelter under my parent's roof and have their help with my daughters. There was a great deal of quality time we shared through a very difficult time personally and professionally that otherwise would not have existed. *Make the most of every opportunity.*

In August of 2020, with the help of my parents, I was able to purchase a home. The house was for sale by owner and was a fixer upper. I was on a shoestring budget and since I was raised within a "handy" family, I wasn't afraid of the work that needed to be done to make it livable by my standards (which of course, are higher than most). My dad was a retired carpenter. My mom was a good painter. I had tackled many home improvement projects and had just gotten done planning and overseeing a $300,000 remodel at the law firm. I knew I could do this!

The remodeling work was literally therapy for me.

Due to the pandemic, we were still working virtually, so I would run the law firm by day 60 hours a week and then remodel my house every night from 8 pm until the wee hours of the morning and every weekend. The remodeling work was literally therapy for me. I loved figuring out how to fix something, plan the project, budget how much it would cost, and roll up my sleeves to get it done. I decided to blog the entire remodel, which was also part of my therapy. I called it Cheaper Than Wine (cheaperthanwine.com), with the underlying theory that if I wasn't remodeling my house every night, I'd be drinking a bottle of wine instead and so, therefore, remodeling the house was cheaper (and healthier!). Turns out it wasn't cheaper, and I still drank wine, but I had a blast doing it, had such a tremendous feeling of accomplishment, and didn't end up in AA, so I consider it a huge success!

Out of my remodel I also gained confidence, a beautiful home, and a house my girls love living in. They learned that their mom can fix anything. They helped on many projects, and I hope they learned that they can figure out how to fix anything, too!

In the process of remodeling, I realized how much we need women in the trades. Every YouTube video I watched featured men. There were tens of thousands of women out of work during COVID who were quite capable of working in the trades, but we don't have a

35

culture that fully supports it. Increasing the number of women in the trades to a meaningful degree is going to take a heavy lift.

There will be three million jobs open in the trades by 2025. If we think it's difficult to come by qualified contractors, electricians and plumbers now, just wait a couple more years for an even greater deficit in skilled labor with baby boomers retiring. As a society, we have been overly successful in sending nearly every high school graduate to college over the past 35 years. It didn't matter whether they had a plan or the money. Ask those students who graduated from college between 2008-2011, if they wished they would have taken a different course and many of them will say, "yes." When students go to college who aren't prepared, they not only incur debt, but they also miss out on four years worth of earnings. This is a significant opportunity cost. Some people say you need the college years to "grow up," and I would argue that you will grow up pretty darn fast if you live in an apartment and have to start paying your own bills regardless of whether or not you are in school.

I don't know yet how I am going to help solve this not-so-small problem, and know with 100% confidence that I was put on this earth to figure it out and if there is one other thing I know, it's that I can figure out anything. We must shift the paradigm to value education in the trades as much as we do a four-year degree and we must be consciously inclusive of women and the LGTBQIA+ community in the trades culture. I realized I had to first figure out a way to change my career and exit law firm management in order to change the world!

By April of 2021, I was about 85% of the way done with the interior of my house that now looked brand, yet I came home every day to the exterior that still looked like the 50 years old it was. I wanted to improve my curb appeal, but I was out of time, money, and energy. I decided the best way to make a fairly quick, low-cost improvement was to paint the garage, the front door, and update the house numbers that were old and half falling off above the garage door. I was on a mission straight to Pinterest, Google, and Etsy to find a modern house number sign to do the job. I found a house sign with a little planter box that I liked, but I thought, "It's too small to grow anything in there and because it's so small, I'm going to have to water it twice a day. Do I have time for that? Hell no!" I still loved it and wanted one.

Knowing that I had everything in my garage, I built it, I painted it, and found the perfect modern house numbers.

As it was two weeks before Easter, I went to the big box craft store and stood there for an hour in the artificial flower department trying to figure out what I was going to put in the planter box. My spend of $37.15 included a full-size bag of moss, three foam blocks because they don't sell them individually, and an entire bunch of tulips when I only needed three. Also included were twelve bird eggs as again, I only needed one. Upon arriving home, I had to find my wire cutters for the tulips (seriously, they always seem to be missing!), figure out how to make the one robin egg not blow away, and tear apart the Spanish moss to get the handful I needed. Another hour later in design, assembly and clean up (the moss was everywhere), I had the cutest sign ever! And then, I realized Easter was over in two weeks, I thought, oh dear God, what time-suck did I just create with this thing up on my house that I know I will want to update every holiday and season? And in nearly the same breath, I thought, oh thank you God…I had just created my future.

The term "mind blown," was my literal stage for the next 48 hours. In this time, I created an entire company capable of making millions in my head. I realized everybody had a front door. Some people need house numbers. Some people may want their last name. Some people may want a monogram. Some people need vertical signs or horizontal ones. And what about the people who lived in apartments, condos, and assisted living facilities? They had a front door, too. This was my answer to owning my own company, moving out of law firm management, and getting women into the trades. Wow. *Opportunities to shine exist all around us and life is all about what you make of it.*

The first person I shared my prototype and idea with was my mother. She has always been my litmus test. She is never afraid to speak her mind whether I want to hear it or not and have always admired her for her honesty. I always know where I stand with my mom. Someday, I hope my girls call me first, too. Much to my surprise when I told my mom about my idea to start a company, she said, "I think it's great. I'll be happy to help you when I retire next month." What?! I didn't think that she would say that. I thought, "Well, I guess

I'm going to have to figure out how to start a company while running a law firm, finishing my remodel, and trying to be a great mom." I knew it was going to come at a great monetary, physical, mental, and emotional expense, but I've never been one to say no, so I thought to myself, let's do this!

I immediately decided that I knew how to run a multi-million-dollar company with my eyes shut and hands tied behind my back, but I had NO idea how to start one. I am not suggesting managing a company is easy, but I fundamentally understood that running an established company and starting a company from the ground up were two very different things and no amount of my education or experience could prepare me for the difficult journey.

I hired a business coach, who specializes in helping small to medium size businesses with systems and sales processes. In two weeks, we came up with a name, a tagline, and secured a domain. I built a rudimentary website with the help of a wonderful expert. Hopefully, you're noticing a common thread of "I don't work alone." Most leaders know that you should hire terrific people around you that are smarter than you are and let them do their job! Know your role. Delegate the rest. Does it cost money? Yes. Is it worth it? Yes. The key is hiring the right business partners and being strategic about what, when, and who you outsource to.

The next step was to do some market research for product viability and pricing before I spent too much more time or money going down the wrong path. Making our Entry Envy brand sign by hand with my new Cricut machine at 4 AM the night before, we entered a craft fair. We took five sample signs and in less than six hours, we captured nearly 250 email addresses from interested prospects. We were on our way.

I knew I had a viable business on my hands. The next step was the confidence I needed to quit my day job. I started working with another coach, who counseled me saying that Entry Envy would never be as successful as it could be unless I gave it 100%. Giving it 100% required me to quit my day job. His remarks, "Don't quit your job when you've replaced your income; quit your job when you know *how* to replace your income." That statement made a huge impact in my direction. *Play the cards you're dealt to the very best of your ability.*

I did not have a job that was a "two-week notice" type of position. I was going to have to give 30 days minimum, probably 60 days, and possibly 90. I knew it was time for me to jump to the other side of the shore. I went through my financials and talked to my bank. I figured out that I could live for at least one year without a single sale from my new company if I pulled every monetary resource that I had available. I would need to use every last penny to bootstrap the company and live until we reached "the black." I determined, one year was my deadline to make it, break it, or bring in investors. High risk? Yes. Calculated? Yes. I decided that there was never going to be a good time to quit six-figure position as a single mom with two kids and chase a dream. Never. So why in the hell not now? And so I did. I gave notice on December 30, 2021. I toasted to the New Year and my next chapter on a boat in Key West overlooking the final sunset of 2021 with one of my best friends and mentor. There was nowhere I would have rather been.

My chosen word of the year for 2022 was **Fearless**.

"Fear kills more dreams than failure ever will." Susy Kassem

I had no business turning my notice in when I did; it was sheer gut, and yet I'm so glad I did because the business started really taking off at the end of February 2022 and my law firm career always carried a demanding workload. Between the two companies, I was already working 130 hours a week and I was doing 200+ hours' worth of work in those 130 hours. My last day at the law firm was officially March 31, 2022.

> "*Fear kills more dreams than failure ever will.*"
> —*Susy Kassem*

I could feel myself slipping off the cliff. I recognized that I was at a point where I couldn't sustain this pace much longer. I wasn't sleeping enough, I often forgot to eat, I wasn't working out as much as I mentally needed to, and my brain was in overload. I know I'm always "okay" if I can see the light at the end of the tunnel during a major project. But when I can't see the light, I panic, and I was approaching panic mode at lightning speed.

Every leadership expert says the most important quality of a leader is self-awareness. I know myself well. I have been a student of myself as much as I have been in my life, career, and education. Extremely high-performing individuals are often addicted to something, in my case, I'm a workaholic. I'm addicted to accomplishment, success, deadlines, and pressure. I started journaling and taking just a few minutes a day for myself. It might have just been one or two minutes outside for a breath of fresh air, but it was something. As of April 1, 2022, with the law firm behind me, I realized that I was entirely in charge of my life. My calendar, my finances, my deadlines. Talk about the word "responsibility." I am the hardest boss I have ever had. I am the one who thinks it's never enough. That I am not enough.

I am continuing to do the deep inner work it will take to overcome this. I have lived my entire life as a "when I" statement. When I graduate from high school, when I graduate from college, when I get married, when I have kids, when I make a million dollars, etc. This hit home hardest in June 2022, when The Subscription Trade Association awarded us Best New Subscription of the Year, just eight months after launching. What more could I possibly ask for? And yet, for me, that award and recognition simply moved the goal posts down the field another 50 yards. It felt like more pressure to live up to. When is enough, enough? I don't know the answer yet, but I know it's not about money; it's about inner peace, satisfaction, happiness, and freedom.

I am the hardest boss I have ever had.

I mastered *fearless*, my word of the year, mid-year through 2022. I'm not afraid, although "the fear" is always just around a dark corner, and I choose to keep walking through the fire. I refuse to be scared. I refuse to believe this company will fail. It's just like jumping off a high dive – I might be scared, but I'd do it anyway. I have all the resources around me that I need, people who believe in me, friends that love me, customers who rave about Entry Envy, and I just keep repeating "Do not be afraid." The Bible says this phrase 365 times; God wants us to live every day fearless. This leads to me my second word of 2022: **Trust**. Trust God, trust the universe, trust the people around me, and trust myself. I've got this. Even if things have not gone the way I thought they would or I perhaps wanted to in times of my life, they turned out better. God has never failed me, and I am 100% confident that He will not fail me now or ever.

"Real courage is being afraid but doing it anyway." Oprah Winfrey

I'm in the startup world and I'm moving fast, loving life, and would not change a thing! I still don't know how my story is going to turn out and I don't want to know, because it would ruin the ending. There are times that I think about turning back. I had a friend recently ask me, "how do you do it all? Not only do it, but do it well and make it look easy?" What others see and what I feel are often not the same, but nonetheless, this was a gracious question, and she wanted a serious answer. I have a quote from Regina Brett on my wall that I look at every morning, *"Get up, dress up, show up."* This is my answer. No matter what. I have always gotten up, put myself together whether I was going to the grocery store or to a job interview, and shown up with a smile on my face ready to face whatever was ahead. It's not always easy and I definitely don't always "feel like it," but as Rose Tremain said, "Life is not a dress rehearsal." We only get to do this once and I live every day with intention and will leave this world a better place than I found it.

> *"Real courage is being afraid but doing it anyway."*
> *– Oprah Winfrey*

This book was written for my daughters and in honor of my mother and father. I am raising my daughters to be level-headed, independent, exude confidence, show kindness, and have grit.

Linda's Wisdom Wrap-Up

Taking the biggest risks will give you the greatest rewards. If you don't show up, you will not succeed.

KIM KELLER

STEP OUT OF EXCUSES

You can, you have, and you will.

I am always amazed at my daughter, Alex, a self-driven student-athlete, who has logged numerous successes in her seventeen years. She has been a straight-A student her entire life, with the exception of a B maybe in 4th grade, and achieved the high honor of blackbelt at age fourteen. She won a county-wide speech contest and brought home ribbons from her STEM fair. She became a competition-level cheerleader in under two years. Despite all this, Alex will be the first to tell you that she's rarely the smartest in the room or the most athletic on her teams, but because she is the hardest working, she is usually the most successful.

At the genesis of the pandemic, with an abundance of time and uncertainty on my hands, I, like so many others, had a thirst for a purpose or a project. I was a forty-something single mom, employed in a "safe" job, generating acceptable work output. I'm outgoing, so I know how and when to speak up, I stayed "active enough", walking my dog through the neighborhoods and maintaining an average body weight. However, in looking at my amazing daughter, I recognized that I needed a purpose and a shift in my thoughts to obtain a stimulating life!

Throughout her childhood, I've posted dozens of Alex's achievements on my Facebook page. I create clever captions and I sport "Taekwondo Mom" shirts every time she attends a tournament.

Most of my postings pertain specifically to Alex and her wins. So, in that same moment of honesty in 2020, while scrolling through our pictures on my page, I realized the difference between us was our mindsets. Alex truly has been raised with a growth mindset.

The concept of a growth mindset had begun to catch fire within my industry around 2018. Our company even championed growth mindset as one of our core corporate values of 2020, along with fearlessness and diversity. At the time, I grasped the general contrast between growth and fixed mindsets. I understood that mindsets are established at a young age, but I had only scratched the surface. As I considered the context of my daughter and her successes, I wanted to understand how my own lifelong fixed mindset had influenced my responses to challenges along the way and even limited my potential in all areas of my life.

As a result of my hesitancy to take risks, I would make excuses for myself instead of stepping out.

I began to dig further into my own history and quickly exposed a life-long habit of celebrating or being envious of my accomplished siblings without undertaking the risk of similar challenges myself. My family contained lawyers, engineers, rescue squad volunteers, and bosses. I had developed a fixed mindset as the youngest of five kids, which meant I doubted my chances at success. As a result of my hesitancy to take risks, I would make excuses for myself instead of stepping out.

Through the study of growth mindset, I can see that I lowered expectations for myself because I didn't think greatness was expected of me. The labels I believed about myself were my crutch. I was accepted to an average university with unremarkable SAT scores. I planned to study radio and TV when a great opportunity emerged at our local CBS affiliate, but because I had a debilitating fear of public speaking, I modified my dream job to working behind the camera as a production assistant, failing completely to realize my dream to become an on-camera reporter/anchor.

I believe we develop an established collection of beliefs at a very young age as a response to the messages we receive from people around us (parents, teachers, etc.). We accept these "little lies" as facts: "She's the brain"; "He's tall so he will make a great basketball player"; "Her mom was musical therefore she will be a great musician"; "My dad was lousy at STEM, so I will be also."

I read when interviewed, Michael Jordan's coaches explained that he wasn't actually the best athlete they had recruited. He was the most coachable and spent the most time focusing on his weaknesses and practicing relentlessly. I recalled my lifelong fear of practicing anything for the very first time – that paralyzing fear that I would showcase my lack of skill. My career-limiting fear of public speaking was particularly hard to face, but it was a fear I needed to overcome.

During the time confined to my home during the pandemic, I made a commitment to myself to seek out small opportunities to practice something new until it was no longer new to me. I actively listened for fixed mindset thoughts that I heard myself saying in my mind. Each of these became a project and a purpose for a personal challenge of mine

I was trying on a growth mindset for size, even if only for a short while. I endeavored to prove myself wrong by trying out a method called "I Think I Can't". I grabbed a sheet of paper and wrote down my plan: I think I can't: Bake a professional-looking Christmas Tree cake

- Why do I think I can't?
  - I've never done it before. I don't have the experience or tools.
- What should I try?
  - Take the time to study best practices from seasoned bakers
  - Refer to tried and true recipes from trusted sources.
- What are my fears / perceived limitations?
  - The great bakers in the family might make me feel self-conscious
  - Hurtful criticism from others.
  - Fear of not measuring up to the great bakers in the family (my mom's cakes were so beautiful, and my sister worked in a bakery and then for Pillsbury).
  - I think I might burn it, break it, waste money on it, or feel like I wasted time.

- How will I keep those from standing in my way/what are my options?
  - Identify great bakers in my life, tell them what I plan to do, and ask them to mentor me or facetime with me during the process
  - Watch baking videos online and on TV
  - Shop at craft stores for professional baking tools, ask for advice and shopping lists
  - Buy two cake mixes! One to break and one to make. This is key! Expect the unexpected!
- Who is my support team?
  - My sister and my friend for both accountability and advice.
  - My daughter for her encouragement and growth mindset to keep me positive.
  - Baking blogs and forums where I can join others to share in my process and success

Documenting the "I think I can't plan" is effective because it forces us to visualize the inevitable bumps in the road, and proactively develop mitigation strategies to deal with them. Furthermore, the anxiety of trying something new is greatly reduced because we have a plan to refer to when stuff happens. Since adopting a growth mindset lifestyle, when faced with new obstacles my daughter and I instinctively look at each other and say aloud, **"WTP (What's the Plan?) followed by O? (Options)? and finally DTDT (Do The Damn Thing!)"**

So, in case you're wondering, I'm so glad I bought that second cake mix. The first cake broke when I flipped it out of the pan. Before allowing myself to feel discouraged, or give up, I referred to my support team as documented in the plan. My daughter offered me some advice. Rather than disposing of the broken cake, Alex said, **"Mom, when you mess it up, dress it up."** She reminded me of the value of practice and suggested **I make a masterpiece out of the mistake.**

We reviewed the plan again, which guided us to baking blogs. The blogs revealed many creative uses for broken cake! Within an hour we had a stunning masterpiece – a layered mint Oreo cake trifle, and a batch of decadent cake pops. We were delighted with the outcome, but we weren't done. We referred to the plan again and reached out to our support team for advice to ensure the second cake would slide perfectly out of the tree-shaped pan. With a few tweaks to the oven temperature and the cake mold, we were back in business. Over the next few months, I followed the plan as my skills improved. I baked dozens of heart cakes for Valentine's Day and Football shaped cakes for Super Bowl Sunday. Each was crafted with more precision and artistry than the last.

Through consistent repetition of a given task, humans begin to perform that task with more precision and speed than before.

In 2020, I executed four "I think I can't" plans. I became a baker! I rewired my brain to dispel the little lie that told me I couldn't do it. I no longer needed a handyman to assemble furniture. I constructed every single piece of furniture in my new condo without assistance. I don't rely on florists to make our arrangements, and I saved much money! I joined a network called Bombshell Fitness. My trainer holds me accountable for explosive intensity in the gym. People have high expectations of me, and I know how to deliver. When I catch myself in a fixed mindset moment, I pivot to WTP, O, and DTDT.

There is an entire science behind the concept of practice called neuroplasticity. The study of neuroplasticity explains that through consistent repetition of a given task, humans begin to perform that task with more precision and speed than before. My daughter is a martial artist and a cheerleader. When she prepares for her sporting events, we often say, "The only bad practice is the one that didn't happen." Her mental practice includes viewing slow-motion videos of herself to examine her technique and form. She also runs through her routines in her mind and compares them to the styles of renowned athletes for tips. How you train your mind is your decision, so make the right one.

Allow yourself time in the process of practice, and only worry about what is within your control.

My daughter began training to be a cheerleader late in life, at the age of fourteen. A back handspring is a minimum tumbling requirement for her high school team. During the spring of 2020, Alex only had five months to learn a back handspring. First, she had to master a handstand, a cartwheel, and a roundoff. Pressed for time, her coach gave her some advice that she carries with her to this day. He said, "In life if the new back handspring that you're working on is still a little wonky, I'd rather you throw the most beautiful cartwheel in the world. After that, focus on the other elements of cheer that are within your control: clean movements, loud spiriting, a positive attitude, and exceptional grades." She made the team!

While there is great value in the statement that "the only bad practice is the one that didn't happen," I recommend taking that up a notch. This year with a growth mindset we have challenged ourselves to elevate our approach to practice. Imagine your dream destination and all of the exotic foods you would taste when you got there. Visualize the excursions you would arrange. Now imagine your next practice is just like your once-in-a-lifetime destination vacation. Would you sit in your hotel room for a week? Would you order pizza for the room? By envisioning your daily practice as the last, most important practice (vacation) of your life, you will begin to seize opportunities for coaching, critiques, and ultimately break through any physical barriers and self-doubt. Why not enjoy a vacation while practicing what you love? After all, practice doesn't make perfect. Perfect practice makes perfect.

What's the first thing you should do after failure? Show up to practice.

Whether you didn't make the team, or your masterpiece fell apart, show up to practice. This builds grit - the amount of effort you are willing to devote to your passion. You may not completely forget the disappointment from an hour ago, but the sting will begin to fade. Also, this is the best time for you to seek feedback and adjust, while the "failure" is still fresh in your mind.

Do you know who your people are? Do you know who they're not? Part of sustaining a growth mindset is establishing accountability. Surrounding yourself with others who have track records of setting goals and then achieving them is vital. Inform others of your plans and review your progress regularly with them. Get a mentor. Be a mentor. Drive your relationship with your mentor. Show up for your mentee if you are asked and agree to be a mentor.

Begin identifying toxic or jealous people. My daughter and I call these people Po-taters. The term infuses a little bit of humor when we are forced to acknowledge that, unfortunately, sometimes the ones we love most might also be haters. There comes a time, in a moment of realization, that we may never get the support or praise we seek. "Haters gonna hate, Po-taters gonna po-tate." So we share a laugh, and then a sigh, and then we move on from them. Don't continue to seek approval, don't worry about what **they are saying about you. It's important not to hurt your own feelings.**

Know when you've cried enough.

In 2012, I was living in Melbourne, Florida with my daughter, who was seven at the time. The economy was going sideways, and hundreds of homes were in foreclosure. I had very little social life. I had been through a difficult divorce, and my wages at work were stagnant. At one point I looked at the calendar and realized I had cried at least once a day for forty-five days straight. I spoke with therapists and talked to my friends, but a dark cloud seemed to have moved in permanently over my head. I couldn't shake it, but I knew this was not the example I wanted to show my daughter.

I asked myself WTP (What is the Plan)? The answer was clear. I knew I needed to relocate to a booming city to provide a better life for my daughter and myself. I accepted a pivotal position that would jumpstart my career and relocated us to the vibrant city of Tampa, Florida. Upon sharing the news of our new venture with my best friend in

Know when you've cried enough.

Melbourne, to my shock, I was met with her criticism and mockery. She actually said the cold words, "Don't call me when you fall flat on your face." My best friend was exposed as a po-tater!

As an unexpected positive surprise, my acquaintance and now lifetime dear friend Renee, showed up to show her support and even helped me pack and drive the moving truck across the state. She revealed herself to be one of my people for life.

I had no friends or family in Tampa, but I was determined to create a wonderful life. Within two weeks I met some great colleagues who were new to the area as well and eager to call us friends. I quickly established a trusted network of moms who were delighted to show us around. Things were going great. I thrust myself and my daughter into numerous life-altering changes in the span of one season. I changed jobs, sold my home, moved my child, found a new school, and secured an apartment in a zip code I had never traveled to before. To my credit the new job I secured entailed a heavy dose of public speaking. After a decades-long history of stage fright, I was on the road to conquering this fear.

One day, I joined my friend Renee on a fun day trip for her to get a tattoo on her middle finger. She had recently finalized a sad divorce, so she wanted the word "Love" inscribed forever to remind her to never give up on love. I admired her for that mindset and decided to join her by having the word "Brave" inscribed on my middle finger. My plan was to look down at my finger prior to any public speaking engagement.

Since I didn't know anyone in Tampa to give me an encouraging glance from the audience, I would simply take a glimpse of my finger for some inked courage. After a month of unpacking and getting settled into my role, the time was coming when I would have to present. I knew I needed to practice and find opportunities to get comfortable. Since our industry focuses heavily on safety, each meeting kicks off with a safety moment. I looked at my finger and then pushed myself to volunteer as the safety facilitator and lead the crowd in ergonomics stretching. After a while, my speaking engagements became more frequent. They were longer, and the topics were more challenging, but I found them to be easier through practice and neuroplasticity. My anxiety completely dissipated.

I've been in Tampa for nearly ten years now. Through my passion for growth mindset, I have delivered dozens of original workshops across multiple organizations on Mindset, Accountability, and Grit. Over the years my *BRAVE* tattoo has faded so much that it looks like a light bruise that goes largely unnoticed. My daughter recently asked me if I planned to get the word re-inked and I told her no. When she asked me why I simply answered, "Because I don't need it anymore." I am a public speaker. I am a baker. I am a handywoman. I am a florist. I am a woman whose changed mindset has changed her life.

This chapter, and my whole heart
are dedicated to my daughter, Alex.

Linda's Wisdom Wrap-Up

Our children provide valuable mirrors to us of insight if we dare to take the long stare.

SARAH SHOULAK

EXECUTIVE DIRECTOR
CURRY FORD WEST

WISDOM FROM CHAOS

To the young professional who is finally feeling like they have solid footing beneath them, I hope this chapter helps you feel confident about how you're taking charge of your future.

I had an amazing upbringing, though we were constantly moving because of the demands of my mother's career. My mother was an incredibly business-savvy executive, while my dad's talents were primarily creative and humanitarian, teaching me about art, love, and other cultures. Dad stayed at home; mom worked in Corporate America. It was so revolutionary that a local news station did a story on our family. Both my parents taught me the sky was the limit. While this Powerpuff-esque recipe created an intense, yet balanced, blend of right and left-brain abilities, it also left me feeling alone when I didn't clearly fit into any clique in my early years.

In my high school years, I was perceived as too weird for the popular kids, too cool for the nerds, too vanilla for the gays at my exclusive arts high school, but too flamboyant for those at my rural public high school. I didn't mind moving often because it gave me unlimited chances to reinvent myself. This also meant, however, that I never learned the value of longevity and follow-through. I didn't realize it then, but I was slowly becoming a people-pleaser who just wanted to do whatever it took at the moment to just fit in and not rock the boat.

Ironically, when I look back at my life and career, I see a path that feels like swinging on monkey bars - propelling myself forward, while swinging aggressively back-and-forth and hanging on until the pads of my fingers blister, hoping I don't fall. I used to think life was all about being strong and muscling my way through, but there's so much more finesse that I never really understood until I started defining myself as a leader. I set out to understand who I was instead of defining myself by the way others view me.

Do Less and Slow Down

If you want something done right, do it yourself. Isn't that what most people tell you? As a budding overachiever in my early twenties, I think I took that phrase as a challenge. How much could I take on and how many things could I do simultaneously seemed to be my mode of operation. I was a regular "Jill of All Trades."

Over the course of my 20s I'd worked as a professional soccer team's mascot, a waitress, a personal assistant, and a school lunch delivery driver. The thrill of a new challenge was so fun that I didn't mind learning what I needed to learn to be successful at yet another job. I had to keep working while in college, which taught me the art of juggling multiple calendars. One job I took on really shook me to my core and gave me a reality check about what work-life balance should look like…or, rather, what it definitely should not look like.

I set out to understand who I was instead of defining myself by the way others view me.

Candance Albright was an ambitious woman who placed an ad on Craigslist looking for a personal assistant. With my experience as an intern working in several different departments in a corporate office of a major national brand, I thought, "Why not? I'm organized, detail-oriented, and would love the challenge of having something new to tackle every day." Or so I thought.

Candace didn't just have a day job she needed relief from. I'd heard of a "side hustle" before, but this woman had three other companies and a networking group that she was running, and it was overwhelming her; hence the need for the assistant. Since she worked out of her house, I had a new office.

My new boss was trying to take things off her plate, but her management style was to micromanage, which left me feeling pressured and defensive. I was constantly ready for her to criticize anything I did since it clearly wouldn't be up to her standards. I found myself intentionally rushing tasks because it would get me to the point of re-doing it again anyway. With this, I started letting more slide than I should have.

You need to be a strong critical thinker, one who sticks to their guns when challenged.

All of this came to a head when she needed to plan a large trip to Dublin, Ireland to attend a major event with her company. Candance asked me to book her trip and was insistent that I use her travel rewards to get the best deal possible. I booked her trip and got her entire trip covered by the travel rewards and she was ecstatic. It seemed like a job well done, until she realized that I had booked the non-refundable trip to Dublin, Ohio, NOT Dublin, Ireland.

Needless to say, we didn't work together much longer after that incident. However I realized a few powerful lessons from that experience: (1) When you are micromanaged, it makes it difficult to complete tasks to satisfaction; (2) Less work gives you greater workplace happiness; (3) It never pays to rush. You can take a little more time to be diligent and make sure all is accurate before you stumble into a challenging situation because you tried to hurry through it.

Attention Doesn't Mean They Like You

While moving around frequently as a child taught me the power of learning to be flexible, I think I confused positive affirmation for actual friendship and closeness, never really defining it fully for myself. I would dye my hair, or dress up in strange clothes, or whatever I thought would make me fit in at the new school or job.

While you should be relatable enough to connect with your co-workers and other people around you, you also shouldn't be like Gumby, bending to anything and everything requested of you. You need to be a strong critical thinker, one who sticks to their guns when challenged. We've all seen that type of manager who "wants to be everyone's friend" and tries too hard to be cool and then seems immature and untrustworthy.

When I was a professor at a local college and would teach Interpersonal Communication and the Fundamentals of Speech, I wanted to help my students understand that they might hear information and need to determine its validity in a presentation or determine if it was just casual conversations. Checking sources was helpful, but there was an element of *personal belief* that went into the decision as well. You should be able to disagree with information if you believe strongly in opposition. You also need to understand where your belief comes from. This is intuition or "trusting your gut."

I would often tell my students, "I don't care who you vote for, how you pray, what you eat, where you live, or how you dress. I want you to know **why** you made those decisions." Sometimes we subliminally accept assumptions or belief systems because they're handed down or come from the environments where we were raised.

All of those years, I thought I was being cool and spontaneous reinventing myself. I was just trying so hard to act a certain way until I realized it was much more important to be authentic at the risk of being disliked than it was to be liked for inauthentic reasons.

I Can Go Anywhere

It doesn't seem like a far leap to think that a people-pleasing attitude may also pair well with a drinking problem. My escape using alcohol was part of my life in my late twenties. In the overscheduled work life I created, I was drinking bottles of wine and downing strong cocktails nightly to balance the amount of production I was accomplishing. I'd balance hours in a graduate school classroom with hours taking shots on a karaoke stage in a local bar.

I wasn't relaxing, I was numbing. I wasn't bonding and spending quality time with friends, I was getting hammered. The work was still getting accomplished, so I believed I was managing it. By the time I turned twenty-seven, I had had occasional experiences with drugs which became more common when I'd overindulge with my drinking. I felt like something needed to change for me. I did not like the direction I was heading. I wanted to stay on the path I wanted my life to be on, so I began attending *Alcoholics Anonymous.*

While the program wasn't for me long-term, some of the lessons I learned during this time in my life did resonate. One person emphasized, "Your rock bottom is when you stop digging." I needed to hear that because I had always been shown dramatic examples of alcoholism in my life and then had people huddled around me saying, "You're nothing like THAT." What I needed to know was, "It's okay to be done with anything you want to be done with, whenever you choose to be done with it."

That became my new hyper fixation. I became obsessed with the idea that I could control my own sobriety in a world where it feels like we can control less and less of our lives. We can't control the weather, but we can impact the climate with our behaviors. We can't control traffic, but we can choose to bike or use public transportation. I may not be able to heal all my traumas and issues overnight, but I can choose to not drink today.

"If I can do that, what else can I do?"

At the end of 2022, I'll have been sober for five years. They try to tell you to take it one day at a time, but there's something encouraging about working your way up to a milestone, like getting excited for a special occasion. I'm giddy. I've never been prouder of myself except for when I purchased my first home. For me, it's not about the alcohol, it's about the feeling of control and positive influence on my own life.

Sometimes, people don't like working out because it can feel like it requires so much work before you see any results, but that's what sobriety feels like. In general, I don't normally feel too many daily or immediate benefits, but then I look at my bank account and my annual doctor appointment notes and remember that it's about the journey.

What I love most is that we all have this power, if you choose to make it about sobriety or commitment to any goal. Discipline is such a powerful skill that can be transferred into so many areas of our life. If you try it, you'll start saying, "If I can do that, what else can I do?"

I'm Sorry, No, I'm Not Sorry

I mentioned earlier that we don't realize the muscle-memory we have until we're put into a new environment. Sometimes, even when we are put into a new environment, we'll fall into bad habits of both physical and emotional behaviors that can range from biting nails to blowing up over something small.

What I didn't learn when I was moving all over reinventing myself was how to take feedback. People who know me well will likely laugh at that (because it's obvious to them), but it hurts me to admit. When people didn't like me before I didn't care because I was going to be moving anyway.

I would rarely invest time into long term relationships whether they were work colleagues, outside of work friends, or even romantic relationships. The journey of building lasting, deep connections with people was difficult for me and I found it often exhausting. Then, I realized a truth - it wasn't just about making those deep connections with everyone around you or your family members and coworkers. You should work on all relationships that have positives for you in your life.

If you're raised with people-pleasing tendencies you'll feel empathetic towards way too many people way too easily and feel personally attached to every relationship, no matter how small. This could also lead to you feeling guilty any time anyone feels bad or leaves your life, since it will have felt like your job to get them to stay. At a recent conference I attended as part of the Orlando Main Streets, there was a session that referred to such people as "energy vampires." These are people who just suck the energy from you whenever they're around. This was a huge realization in the way I fueled my behaviors. What I now understand is that we need to stop being so scared of saying or feeling things that others may disagree with.

That's All, For Now

I know I'm a strong confident woman and I don't just "play" one on tv. I now understand firsthand, that faking it until I made it was exhausting and I realized that I made so many decisions based on what others wanted me to do and even though I was carving out my own path, I was still indulging in bad habits and not taking proper care of myself.

Writing this chapter, I become more reflective, grateful, and excited for what's next, both in this book and my own story. I appreciate your time and interest if you've read this far, I wish you peace on your journey!

This chapter is dedicated to all the people who helped guide me and supported healthy choices along my journey. True, authentic friendship is hard to find, but those people who can help you grow beyond where you felt like you belonged are invaluable.

Linda's Wisdom Wrap-Up

We are capable of just about anything once we can work through understanding ourselves.

DEBORA PORATH

INDEPENDENT SALES DIRECTOR
MARY KAY, INC.

I SAID NO 7 TIMES

I dedicate this chapter to those who have a
burning passion that needs starting! Just jump!

The first piece of wisdom I want to share is one I found while working at Ashland Chemical Company many years ago. I'll never forget that day when the vice president of the company and I struck up a conversation in front of the elevator on the fifth floor. I do not even remember how the conversation started, but to this day I remember how it ended! He said, "There never is a reason to complain. If you do not like something, then change it!"

This piece of advice seemed to hit me right between the eyes! It was so simple, yet so logical. This simple comment from my manager came to mean the world to me, and I guess you could say it became my mantra for how I lived my life.

Fast forward, and I was fifteen years into my career and still loving my job at Ashland Chemical when I was approached twice a day by Jill Kennedy, our mail delivery person, asking me to listen to her talk about a Mary Kay opportunity. My response was no seven times! I looked at my life and thought I had it all. The perfect job, five weeks paid vacation, yearly income increases, exercise twice daily, and I lived a financially fit lifestyle. What did I need with a side gig?

Then one day, Jill knew exactly what to say to change my mind. She said she needed me to go with her to attend a get-together with a group of women, as she was afraid to face a room full of strangers. That cry for help was enough for me to say 'yes' at last. It took us about forty-five minutes to get there and during the drive, Jill began telling me about Mary Kay Ash. During this discussion, she got so emotional she began to cry. I remember thinking, it was so weird, and I said you're crying about a woman? I was equally unimpressed as I walked into the meeting, and to me, they all seemed fairly humdrum. To my surprise, by the end of the meeting, everybody was happy and excited, and they were all sitting up straighter with their shoulders back. The room was filled with positive energy that was nearly palpable!

While observing all this positivity was great, the real clincher for me was when one of the leaders got up and shared how she made $100,000 in her first year! This fact made me take things a bit more seriously. It prompted me to make an appointment for a follow-up meeting with this leader. As I attended my first Mary Kay event, I was amazed at the products, and the wonderful women who were part of this organization, but most of all the wisdom of the creator Mary Kay Ash herself.

Even with being impressed with MK, at my second meeting with the leader, I tried every excuse in the book to convey how this was not the opportunity for me. For instance, I said I had never tried anything like this before, I've never 'done' makeup or skincare. This leader had an answer for all my objections but better yet, she challenged me to give it a year. So, I did, and in less than a year, I was so busy that I became known as the Mary Kay lady at Ashland Chemical.

The room was filled with positive energy that was nearly palpable!

Even though my Mary Kay business was blossoming, I still saw it as just a side gig, and while I began to build a team and started making money, my main job was still at Ashland. However, my love for this job began to fade when the company was acquired in an acquisition, and the new company began taking over management positions and making changes to the entire culture of the company. I felt like I had truly hit the 'glass ceiling', and on top of that, it seemed that someone would have to retire (or die!) for my career to advance. But I still loved my job, so I stayed.

Fast forward a year or so, and my new boss from the acquisition thought I needed a challenge so before we sat down to complete a performance appraisal, he informed me I wouldn't be getting a "4." (Grade level 4 in a performance appraisal is excellent and a 5 would be walking on water and I've been told no one ever received a 5). So, why was this a shock? Well, the bottom line was this – if someone received a 3, 2 or 1 on a performance review, they knew they would not be working at Ashland Chemical for long!

As the company began to change and after the new management's performance appraisal process was very unfair, my heart sank into my stomach and instantly my intuition told me that I should put in my two weeks' notice and pursue this new part-time business. No one could believe that I would really resign from a sixteen-year career to pursue an executive position in what was usually considered to be a 'side gig'. In an elevator full of employees someone asked me, "Is it really true!?" And, yes, it was true – I had taken the leap off the corporate ladder right into the organization called Mary Kay!

God knows when to allow what we may see as a negative to push us toward our destiny.

While everyone else seemed to see it as a negative, I knew that God knows when to allow what we may see as a negative to push us toward our destiny. I always believed that if you took a leap of faith, He would give you peace in your decision. I hung onto that one nugget of advice: don't complain. If you do not like something, then change it!"

When I first joined Mary Kay, I could not talk in front of people. I had to work through this, and I came to the realization it's not about me. It's about the people needing to hear from me. I can just try to look the best and be the best and I'm there for them. That takes me out of the scenario, and it makes me so proud when I hear a client say, "I feel pretty for the first time" and I know I had a hand in making her feel that way.

I found myself sharing this wisdom with my mom recently. I believe she needed to hear from me as my dad passed away over two years ago, but my mom still cries every day. I encouraged her to take her mind off her sadness by helping someone else, thinking about others, and getting involved in the community. When you take the time to care for someone else, you don't have the time to feel sorry for yourself.

I was living in Ohio at the time, and I really began to concentrate on making my 'side hustle' my full-time focus. So I turned myself into a sponge to absorb all the training, I could get. I heard someone once say that if you took all the classes that MK had to offer, you would have the equivalent of a Ph.D.. My focus really began to pay off, and I began building a large team. I was a self-starter and motivator that loves a challenge, and the transition from corporate to independent business owner provided me with many opportunities to grow. Along with the growth was also a newfound freedom. Freedom to be my own boss and write my own schedule.

You should give anyone with a negative attitude extra attention – so I piled it on!

One of the things I really enjoyed about my new business was the ability to change people's minds. For example, I had a woman who had her arm twisted to come to my house for an event, by her sister and it was evident she was NOT into being there. So, I asked her, "Are you okay?" She said, "Well, my sister dragged me here." I took this as a challenge. One of the things I had learned was that you should give anyone with a negative attitude extra attention – so I piled it on! By the end of the evening, she had a smile on her face, and she became one of my best clients. This was my realization of the power of positivity in action.

While I really enjoyed my large team in Ohio, I began to notice that no one was 'passing' me and growing beyond where I was. This is one of the things I learned in management training, you always want your team to do better than you so they move up the ladder of success. I would assure my team that there were always enough clients for all of us and that certain people will connect with others because of their personalities. It's not always about the products. It is also about how you make your clients feel.

I continued with my power of positivity, both with my team and with my clients. Of course, I was also enjoying the freedom that working for myself gave me. Soon my freedom turned into a necessity. Like most women, I wanted a child. My daughter Liana Elizabeth was born with special needs that require complete and twenty-four-hour total care, and I found that by being my own boss I was able to provide what she needed. A fact that would NOT have been the case if I had stayed in my corporate job.

When something this life-altering happens, human nature can take over and push you to say, "Why me?" I did not choose this mindset; I accepted the gift of having my daughter. Liana Elizabeth is an amazing human being, and I am honored to be her mother. While others might convey to me that they couldn't "do what I do," or believe it is difficult, I look at her as a gift from God. I believe she is a positive in my life, as I'm never alone and I have what most people never find, which is a "forever friend." My daughter's gifts to me are beyond her smiles, hugs, and "I love yous". I know we all have a purpose. Liana has a purpose. I have a purpose. You have a purpose. Liana doesn't define me, and I do not define her. No purpose is lesser or greater than anyone else's. I felt that my purpose was to be Liana's mom and to lead a group of amazing women to become successful as Mary Kay Consultants.

As much as I understand that we all have a purpose, there's a constant nudging that goes on in a person's life when you aren't focused on your destiny and don't know your purpose. The reason I say this is to share another lesson I learned when looking at the "dash." Have you ever heard the adage that when you look at a gravestone, there is a birth year, and a year of death, and there usually is a dash between those two dates – and the ultimate question is, what did you do with the dash? What did you do with your time between birth and death? Have you ever asked yourself why it is taking me so long to move forward, or why are others getting ahead faster? What do they know about their "dash" that you might not know?

What do they know about their "dash" that you might not know?

As I just turned sixty years old, I know time is ticking and to complete my business passion in time before a forced retirement at age sixty-five, my activity needs to increase and be consistent, and I need to concentrate on what the final lap of my 'dash' is going to look like. I want to make sure I always stay focused with a positive attitude.

In the journey of the "dash" you push through to win battles within your mind that would hold you back. You also need to approach life with a positive attitude and be willing to make changes instead of complaining about the 'status quo'.

My wish for everyone reading my story is to act upon your passion and complete your "dash" with a fulfilling journey of growth, believing strongly that differences can be made one face at a time. Because I am a girl from West Virginia. I tell the truth. I tell it like it is. I work hard for what I want, but most importantly I love people and I want the best for them. I just hope that by sharing my story and a few pearls of wisdom, I can make a difference!

I dedicate this chapter to my forever friend Liana Porath.
Every day of your life is God's manifested love to me.

Linda's Wisdom Wrap-Up

What are you doing with your dash? Life isn't the destination it is the journey.

ERIN FELDMAN

SUCCESS IS NEVER FINAL, FAILURE ISN'T FATAL

Dedicated to all of the wanderers out there who think they are lost and need to be found. Love and compassion are unlimited resources, starting with yourself.

I've always said I've won the genetic lottery by being born into my family. I had nothing to do with this…there was never anything I could do about who'd be my family. Yet, I won this lottery. I come from good stock. Growing up, we were not that well off. I come from a hard-working, middle-class family. Though we never had an excess of money, we never wanted for anything, and we had all we needed. Winning the genetic lottery is where my story begins—but this is just the beginning—my origin story…

My adult story starts when I was a young schoolteacher. I was driving forty-five minutes to work and back every day and making a teacher's wage when I was given the opportunity to quit that job and work across the street from where I lived, dropping my commute to just a few minutes a day. The new opportunity was working in my family's business when we picked up our first big retail client. I was to start at the ground level as an administrative coordinator.

I was given a project to support the contracts we couldn't find in the system from when they were merged over from a previous administrator. Within a few weeks, I'd created a system to pass along the work to the main office, but I had become an extra hand touching it that was unnecessary. The process I had created streamlined the system to help service clients more quickly. This made me more successful and made more money for the company, but I was bored out of my mind because I had simplified the process so much, I had nothing to do!

My boss recognized this, saw my potential, and offered me an outside sales position. This entailed territories and selling across the United States and Canada. To say I rocked it would be an understatement. I reached top sales in formerly dead areas quarter over quarter. Yes, I know I am patting myself on the back, which is something I don't often do. It's only recently that I can recognize my value at all. More about that later.

Fast forward…the company my parents built was a crazy success and I was a part of that success. It was such a great success that they were offered quite a bit of money to sell. This is where winning the genetic lottery comes in. Upon the sale of the company, because it was my family's business, I was awarded a huge lump sum of money. On top of that, I had another large amount of money coming to me from bonuses. I found myself, at the age of twenty-six, with enough money to retire and never work again if I played it right, but I didn't realize that at the time. It was a lot of money, more than most will see in a lifetime, but it wasn't that much money. Again, right place, right time, right family. However, it wasn't that simple. As part of the family money management plan, we hired one company to manage our separate portfolios. Consequently, I was invested money that I had no access to and lived off the interest.

At this point I found myself asking, "Now what?" I really wanted to stay with the company because I enjoyed my job, I was good at it, and I knew how to make money doing it. It felt good to be a success and not be bored. I really didn't feel like I was anything special. I was just doing my job and being great at it. I won every challenge. They'd given me garbage territory and I turned it into the top producer in the nation and I had fun doing it!

As it turned out, to stay was not in the cards. The new ownership didn't want me and started to push me out once the company sale was finalized. At the time I couldn't figure out why they would get rid of their top producer and their reasoning didn't make sense. I ended up resigning in the end because it was made very uncomfortable for me. They gave me lame excuses, but the truth is, they wanted their own team and didn't want the family or me involved in the new company structure. They ended up closing our company and absorbing the business into their own—a large warranty administrator that is well known today.

I was also newly married, so I took it on the chin and went on to the next phase of my life. I was twenty-six and essentially retired. I didn't need to work and have always lacked passion. I still had no idea what I wanted to be when I grew up. I still don't at forty-three. What should I do? I was naïve and young. It never occurred to me that I could travel or spend money or do anything crazy. I just kept my money invested while I tried to figure out what to do with the rest of my life.

Wanting to work, I sent out about 700 resumes. I was overqualified for most jobs but on paper I was underqualified for upper-level positions, even though I felt I could run a company. After much searching, I decided to go into business for myself. Because I always struggled with my weight and fitness and worked at gyms through college, I decided to open my own gym. Unfortunately, it was at the downturn of the 2008-2010 recession. The plaza I was located in closed down, one by one, storefront by storefront, except for the chain grocery store anchor.

I had never really failed at anything in my life until then.

This was devastating to me. I had never really failed at anything in my life until then. This wouldn't be the only failure I experienced, though. My first marriage failed as well. I was separated within ten months and divorced within thirteen, just prior to opening the gym which again, also failed. How ironic to have such great success at the age of twenty-six and follow that with my very first big failures. I went from being on top of the world to feeling lonely and depressed.

It was not long before I met the man who would become my second husband. With him I became a stay-at-home mom of three and PTO president for the subsequent nine years. But that marriage failed as well and I found myself divorced again, out of the workforce for twelve years, with three small kids.

I was shunned by my community following my divorce. It was then that I found out who my true friends were. I went from being number one, throwing backyard parties for 200-300 people, having a million "friends", a perfect family, an idyllic life (on paper), to a new neighborhood, a new house, and still no passion or direction.

That's when my self-deprecation peaked. I was on a downward spiral of self-worth. Others see, and have always seen, the value in me more than I do, and at that point I no longer had external validation. As a result, I developed terrible anxiety – even though I've always felt like I exist in a protected bubble. I don't have to worry about money like most people. I don't really have anything to "worry" about. I always know everything will be okay, but there's the anxiety. It is a physical feeling that I can't trace to a specific worry because I truly never feel like anything bad will happen to me, despite the "failures" and horrible year I had had. It's not healthy. I'm working very hard at healing.

When I turned thirty, my money became more accessible. I broke off from my family's investments. Feeling like a real adult, I went out on my own and found my own investments and investors to work with so I could have my money work more for me. My first investment was real estate. I took about a half million dollars and invested it in several pieces of real estate, realizing 12% profit on my money. I was off to a great start. Currently, I make far more than that as a passive investor in several diversified ventures, though I still don't know what I want to be when I grow up.

I was recently asked if I had a prenuptial agreement with my husband. I did not. The way we split was that what was mine before the marriage was mine. However, when you run any of that money through a joint account with your spouse, it becomes a marital asset, along with the marital home, no matter how it was purchased. Marital assets are split 50/50 in the state of Florida. When you get married, you expect it to be forever. I really wasn't taking any precautionary measures to protect myself, even though I had one failed marriage. I really thought this second one was forever. I can tell you that I have learned a lot. I share this with you not to make you feel sorry for me. Please don't feel sorry for me. I chose my path financially, in my marriage, and ultimately in my divorce. I share this so you may protect yourself from any mishandling of your own money. It is not a sign of selfishness. It is an obligation to yourself and your family to be smart with your assets.

"Not all those who wander are lost."

During the Covid pandemic, I was sitting home, not working, with nothing to do while my kids attended virtual school when I came across an ad for a free three-day manifestation course. I figured, *Why Not? What have I got to lose?* I was positive I'd be "sold" something in the end but maybe I'd get something out of the free part and I wasn't buying anything. During that free three-day, one-hour-a-day course, I discovered the art of manifestation, which unbeknownst to me, I had been using all along. I realized I had been manifesting my whole life without knowing it or harnessing it. This was a life-changing realization. I always thought my life just happened to me, but it turns out I have always subconsciously designed and created my life. The problem was I was often manifesting terrible things for myself just as much as I was manifesting positive things in my life. Having this awareness set me on a new path—and the leader of the course never tried to sell me anything.

It is an obligation to yourself and your family to be smart with your assets

I look back to when I was younger and thought I was lost. I had no idea what I wanted to do with my life. I went to college, but I still had no direction. I was a professional student only because I had no idea what direction I wanted to go in. If there was a major – I tried it. I even took a course called "Serial, Series, and Mass Murderers." Who does that? I had zero direction. I floated along but somehow always knew everything was going to be okay. I just didn't know what path I was going to take. I was wandering, but I wasn't lost. I knew everything would work out one way or another. Call it positive thinking, call it whatever you like. I don't know what to call it. It was just a gut feeling. Manifestation!

I know I am my own worst enemy. I don't like it. I know and have known I needed a change. When I was thirty-nine and about to go through my second divorce, I went through a major midlife crisis. My youngest started Pre-K. I had been heavily involved with the preschool and I knew I wouldn't continue doing so. I was wandering again. I had nothing to do, and I made some terrible choices.

My money was working for me still, and let me make this clear, I didn't retire with enough money to last me the rest of my life. I am smart with my money. I did not overspend or start living like a millionaire. Sure, I had a nice house and didn't want for anything, but, as I stated, I didn't travel the world or buy fancy cars. Thanks to some very good decisions and surrounding myself with the right people, I have been living off the interest of this money since I got it in 2006. I haven't touched the principal except to purchase real assets, which are included in my net worth, which has remained steady.

Where am I today? I have three beautiful kids that I love and adore. I truly have nothing to worry about. I still have a ton of angst and negativity. What am I doing to overcome it? Starting about two years ago, I knew I needed to make a change. I took the manifestation course mentioned previously and before I knew it, I manifested a new man in my life. His name is Chris.

Chris has been the most influential in my process of growing. He recognizes my manifestation, and he tells me I have the Midas Touch—everything I touch turns to gold. He started the ball rolling for me to actually begin making the changes in my mindset. He has made the biggest impact on my life. He has started me on a path of positivity, gratitude, and abundance. These are all changes I want and must make in my life, and to have the support that I do from such a positive force has really been key. He sees the great in me and is helping me to see it as well.

It is no surprise that in the past, I haven't processed good advice, or any advice at all for that matter. I didn't even realize people thought differently than I do until this year. I certainly wasn't hearing any advice anyone gave me. Chris and I went out to Vegas so he could attend a mastermind as a business and transformational coach. My plan was to go to the spa while Chris attended the conference. Just to see what it was all about and, honestly, to tell him it was garbage, with a very closed mind, I decided to join the morning session of the conference. I can tell you I started out with all of my walls up, and my participation level was argumentative and disinterested. Let's just say I wasn't committed to playing at a "level 10." By the end of the first day, however, I was sucked in, and by the end of the second day, I was signing on the dotted line for the year-long program.

This is something I would never have considered in the past. I was opening up; I knew I needed something in my life. I can tell you that this group that I joined and this coach/program have made the second biggest difference in my outlook, my mindset, and my life. I am looking at things differently. I am looking at myself differently. I am looking at others differently. I am more open to change. I'm not going to lie—it is a process. It is a process I need, I want, and a process that is making a difference in my life. Yes, it's uncomfortable at times! I am learning that I need to be comfortable with being uncomfortable. I have realized that I don't want my kids to fall into my past mindset. I want them to have a positive outlook on life. A strong, positive mindset. It will make a huge difference in all of our lives.

My friend Jennifer reiterates that we are the sum of our top five people we hang around. I can tell you that she is absolutely correct. Having Chris in my life with his contagious, positive attitude (yes, it may be annoying at times) and collaborating with my fellow mastermind community in the coaching group, as well as my coach, has changed my mindset and attitude. It is a work in progress and one I am committed to. Happiness is underrated. I deserve to spend this money and time

I am learning that I need to be comfortable with being uncomfortable.

and hard work on myself. I owe it to myself, my family, and those I love. I am thankful to my friend Linda for encouraging me to share my story and become confident in what I have accomplished. I am a work in progress and fortunate for the life I have had and the friends and network I have in my life. I am looking forward to many more accomplishments and personal successes.

If I were to look back on my past fifteen years or so, since I accidentally-on-purpose retired, and pass along my most important pieces of wisdom, I would say it doesn't hurt you or take anything away from you to be nice to people and be positive and you can't have too much love in your life. You don't have less if you give more—you get more. These are infinite resources. My biggest piece of advice or wisdom is, "Don't float! Don't waste time. Take control of your life!" Don't let your life just happen to you. Time is a commodity we will never get back. Figure out your passion now. Wake up! Remember, "Success is not final, and Failure is not fatal".

Dedicated to my children,
discover your passion,
live your truth.

Linda's Wisdom Wrap-Up

We are all manifesting our own lives whether we realize it or not. Be careful what you manifest.

LINDA BRUNS

CHIEF INSPIRATION OFFICER
WOMAN HAVE NEEDS TOO

FOOD AS THY MEDICINE

This chapter is dedicated to those women who know it is time they take their health into their own hands. To you, the reader, it is never too late to take control of your health. You will thank yourself later and you will have a fresh new outlook on life.

Everyone tends to take their health for granted until something major happens! I believe it was the fall of 1990 when I began to experience extreme fatigue. I was riding my bike to work every day, about five miles each way, coming home, cooking dinner, taking care of daily chores, and so on. I got to the point that I was so exhausted that I couldn't get OFF the couch. I just figured I was tired from all I was doing.

During a business road trip with my husband and our collegues who were also friends, the flood gates opened. Thank goodness they had leather seats because I just started bleeding, I had already had my regular menstrual period the week before, so it was odd I was starting again. It wouldn't stop. Nothing was helping. I couldn't get enough protection for myself or anything I happened to be sitting on. It was HORRIBLE, to say the least. Did I mention it was also very embarrassing?

Long story short, it was determined that I have hypothyroidism. This diagnosis from my doctor who is well respected in his field, advised me to go on Synthroid. I told him I did not want to take a pill for the rest of my life, but he said I had no choice. The doctor told me I had no choice. This was the only way. We played with the levels for about a year. It's a tricky thing. With trial and error, we finally found the proper dose for my body and things settled down, and I thought that was the end of it.

Never did anyone tell me that I needed to change my diet, why or how this happens, and what I could do to help myself. I was much younger and naïve at that time. I can tell you I was just happy it wasn't more serious and that I wasn't going to die. Because when I was bleeding on my friend's leather seats, I literally thought I was going to bleed to death. Little did I know at the age of twenty-eight that this was not going to be the end of my issues with my hypothyroidism. It was just the beginning.

Never did anyone tell me that I needed to change my diet.

Growing up the daughter of a physical education teacher, I was always on the move. We had a basketball court in our front yard and an obstacle course with trapezes in my backyard. Our house was the playground of all playgrounds. I was fortunate to have parents who enjoyed spending time with us, and our good health was important to them. Playing outside, exerting energy, and enjoying nature were all part of that good health recipe.

Mom always had a home-cooked meal on the table, no later than 6:00pm. My dad was a strong believer that eating after 6:00pm was not good for your body. My mom was very organized and taught us what meal prepping was all about even before meal prepping was a thing. On top of that, if she knew she was going to be home a little late, she would have us start the supper on the stove. Yes, I learned around the age of ten how to cook dinner over the phone. It was fun and exciting and sometimes frustrating. Mom taught me I was capable. She also taught me that if I made a mistake, I was either going to learn from it or learn how to fix it. Either way, she was patient and so was the rest of the family.

Home-cooked meals, there's nothing like them. Especially when your mom knows how to cook. Looking back, I realize how much healthier it was and better tasting than the meals my friends were eating. Most of my friends' parents were cooking out of a box. It reminds me of the Sugar Hill Gang song Rapper's Delight lyrics:

> *Have you ever went over*
> *A friend's house to eat*
> *And the food just ain't no good*
> *I mean, the macaroni soggy, the*
> *Peas are mashed*
> *And the chicken taste like wood...*

I rarely was up for eating at a friend's house for dinner. No one cooked like mama.

Included in creating a healthy lifestyle example for us kids, my mom and dad did not drink alcohol as a habit (maybe an occasional drink when they went out dancing) nor did they smoke and, rarely, said a cuss word. We were far from "Polly Anna," but we were accused of being the *All-American* family. What matters is that we were fortunate to have what we had, a very loving family whose parents taught us to be lovers, not fighters.

My mom's wisdom was: "Your body is your temple. Take care of it and don't let anyone take advantage of you or your body." Dad's wisdom: "Everything in moderation."

Nonetheless, I was conscientious about taking care of my body. I also played a lot of sports and burned a lot of calories. I would have my occasional Pepsi and bag of Doritos to satisfy that craving. I remember when I was in my early 20s, I was running three miles a day and drinking only one Pepsi a day, I still had that little belly bump. I immediately stopped buying Pepsi. I knew if I had it in the house, I would be tempted. I wasn't going to exercise daily and work on being healthy and ruin it with one soda. I learned that if I didn't have it in the house, I couldn't drink it. My discipline improved once I was in the habit of not drinking it. You can put soda and chips in front of me and I don't have to have a sip or even one chip. It definitely comes down to mind over matter.

A very loving family whose parents taught us to be lovers, not fighters.

I was twenty-five years old when I gave birth to my son, a very healthy nine-pound, one ounce perfect baby boy. His birth was a complete natural child birth with no drugs. After his birth in 1988, I remember starting to feel sluggish all the time. I just figured it was because I had a baby and was busy all the time working and taking care of a family.

Fast forward to the embarrassing bleeding event of 1990 and the subsequent thyroid diagnosis, and surprisingly, everything was going along fine for a while after I began taking Synthroid. However, I battled my weight constantly. I just figured it was due to my weekend chips and dip and not exercising as much as I was accustomed to.

A short time later, I got into the hospitality industry as a profession. This was an industry filled with fun people. Good people. I enjoyed my job very much and was making a good life and having a great time with all of it.

A great part of this job was socializing, entertaining, and traveling. I would enjoy beautiful, delicious food, mouth-watering wines, and plenty of vodka, and because of all the socializing, much less workout time. I ALWAYS packed my tennis shoes and workout clothes. ALWAYS, they came home clean and unworn from being on the road.

She was a body reader. She knew more about my body than I did in one hour.

Yes, I realize that this wasn't a healthy lifestyle, even for a completely healthy person. Little did I know that my liver was already compromised due to my hypothyroidism or vice versa. I believed since I was taking my Synthroid, I was status quo and "all good in the hood". My health battle got worse. I did cleanses and low-carb diets to try and help. They did. Temporarily.

I was even going to an acupuncturist (one of the most amazing women I have ever met and an even better acupuncturist!). Without me telling her what I had going on in my body, she told me I had a compromised liver. She was a body reader. She knew more about my body than I did in one hour. Then she told me I needed to stop looking at vodka as a medicine and see it more for what it was - a poison.

By this time, I was divorced after a thirty-two-year marriage, on the road a lot, working long hours, and working out a lot. I had a regimen of going to work, going straight to the gym, and only socially drinking one or two times a week. I never drank at home during the week. Only a drink or two when at dinner with a client. Sometimes more if out with my friends.

I had started a new job and there was a lapse in my insurance. When I went to get my Synthroid prescription filled, I found out it was going to be several hundred dollars a month instead of $37 per month. So, brilliant person that I am, I decided, no problem, I'll just wait until I get my new insurance and go back on my Synthroid.

D-Day arrives, I was out in Vegas for work. It was a long week of working sun-up to sun-down, dinner, and events every night. Lots of yummy food, delicious wine, vodka, and very little sleep. Lots of fun.

On our last night in Vegas (my boyfriend, Tim, who is now my husband, was with me), we were out on the town with friends and industry colleagues. After appetizers and cocktails, I enjoyed a scrumptious seafood platter with muscles, shrimp, and crab. Healthy by anyone else's standards. Then off to a show. I had a glass of wine, one martini, and I was then on my third drink.

Normally we would go out after the show but, I was not feeling well and told Tim I needed to get back to the room. He wanted to do anything he could to help me but, honestly, I did not know what would help me. I didn't know exactly what I was feeling. I wasn't drunk or sick to my stomach. I was just very uncomfortable. After a long walk back to the room, I went straight to bed.

I lay there with my eyes wide open, listening to Tim sleep. I was teetering between calling 911 or just meditating myself to sleep. I felt like my heart was going to pop out of my body. I felt like my entire body was swollen like a blowfish. I had never felt like this before. To say it was scary is just scratching the surface. I finally fell asleep and fortunately, I woke up the next morning. I remember how relieved I was when I woke up. I told Tim, immediately, how scared I was, and he was a little perturbed that I didn't tell him the night before how seriously ill I was feeling.

I was feeling much better but, definitely still not myself. My heart had calmed down a lot but was not quite back to normal. We had plans to go up to Mt. Zion and go hiking. Tim was ready to take me to a hospital, but I assured him I was feeling better, and that we would stick to our plans. It was a fun and beautiful day hiking in the mountains. I couldn't do as much as I wanted, but I was just happy to be alive and enjoying the beauty of Zion with the man I loved.

When I got back home, I made an appointment with a doctor. I had to find a new doctor, as I had just recently moved. New job, new home, new doctor, new health issues. New lease on life because I had survived what I felt was a near-death experience.

It was time for the healing to begin. I met with my new gynecologist, and he ran my thyroid levels and suggested I see an endocrinologist. At this point, I had been home for about three weeks. I explained to him that I was staying with my workout regimen even though my body was still swollen. The area behind my knees was so swollen I couldn't bend my knees properly. I was determined to continue my daily walks, my bike rides, and work out in order to get rid of this poison in my body. I wasn't sure it was poison, that is just how it felt.

I found an endocrinologist I liked. I learned from her that my thyroid levels were responding since I was back on my Synthroid. I asked her where the levels were before, in comparison. She explained to me that when my new gynecologist did my first lab work after Vegas, the levels were so high, they did not even register on the chart. This spoke to me. This told me how foolish I was to think I could go off the Synthroid for a few months and not have any side effects from it.

I had survived what I felt was a near-death experience.

I didn't realize how instrumental it was for my body and how much my body needed it to stay regulated.

The endocrinologist explained that my thyroid was a little swollen. Not abnormally out of range, nonetheless, worth having it checked out. She suggested I see an ear, nose, and throat specialist and also gave me a book to read about diet and autoimmune diseases. This was the first time I learned how important the correlation between diet and autoimmune disease is. I started reading.

I booked an appointment with the ENT and a nutritionist on the same day. I was determined to get to the bottom of my new issues as soon as possible and I was not going to stop at listening to just one or two people. I wanted to hear different views and I had already decided I wanted to find and take the most natural, body healing efforts possible.

The ENT prescribed me something for acid reflux and said I should take it for about a year and see how it goes. I told him I did not want to take a pill to cure my body. I wanted to heal my body as naturally as possible. What are my options? "You have no options. Just do what I say and take this for a year and let's see how you are doing."

"No. Just NO!" I walked out that door and drove straight to my next appointment with the nutritionist. I walked in there with the prescription in hand.

The first thing Sarah, my new nutritionist, asked me was, "Why are you here?" I explained exactly what I had been through and broke down in tears as I told her, "I want to heal my body naturally. I don't want to take a pill. I want to get to the source of my problem and heal my body. I do not want to mask the problem." As my voice started to crack and tears streamed down my face, I told her that I did not want to be like my mother and my grandmother. I had watched them go to the doctor with their aches and pains and before they knew it, they were taking a pill to wake up, a pill to go to sleep, a pill for constipation, a pill for diarrhea, a pill for anxiety, a pill for you name it. Before my grandmother passed, she was taking over twenty pills a day. At the time of this particular appointment, my mother was taking seventeen.

I learned how important the correlation between diet and autoimmune disease is.

I handed Sarah the prescription the ENT gave me and told her this is what he suggests for me, and I don't want to do it. She took one look at it, crumpled it up and threw it in the trash. "Well, we are not doing this. We are going to heal you from the inside out. Food is thy medicine. We will heal you with food." This was music to my ears. Sarah was EXACTLY what my body needed.

So, my health journey began. The *real* health journey. The journey that would be life-changing. Not easy, not simple, not cookie cutter. A true process of elimination. A process of learning and understanding MY body. Figuring out what my body needs, and what it doesn't tolerate.

Yes, alcohol is poison to my body, but it wasn't the only thing that was poison. At the beginning of my journey, I was on protein and greens. I was loving it! I was making fresh frittatas every day. I love to cook so this was exciting for me. I was experimenting with a whole new way of cooking. I never liked eggs growing up. The thought of eating chicken or seafood every morning wasn't appealing. I became a frittata queen! Before I knew it, I had friends and family requesting my frittatas. They were absolutely delish!

Once you make the declaration, make your plan, stick to it, and re-declare it as often as you need to stay on track.

While I thought I was being healthy, unbeknownst to me, I was feeding my body poison! I found out that eggs are poison to my body. I was disappointed. I finally learned how to like and enjoy eggs. Another source of protein. What I did learn was that I was not, am not, allergic to vodka, red wine, eggs, and gluten, among other foods. I'm just intolerant. I am able to have these things once a week and have a limited amount. For the most part, I follow these guidelines. There are times that I throw caution to the wind and overconsume on bread, potatoes, and pasta. When I do, I feel the effects immediately. It reminds me that I have poisoned my body and it is important for me to detox and return to my anti-inflammatory regimen. Most people use the word "diet". I see it as a way of life. A way of life that will make my body happy.

It is amazing to me how we, as humans, know right from wrong, know what we need to do on a daily basis, and still make wrong choices for ourselves. I know what I need to do for my body. It all comes down to a decision. Anything we want to change in our lives comes down to a decision. Once you make the declaration, make your plan, stick to it, and re-declare it as often as you need to stay on track. We are not going to poison our bodies or poison our minds. We are going to create an environment for maximum success in every area of our lives.

Now the fun begins as I am on a quest. I am on a quest to take all the decadent recipes I've loved for so long and learn to create new recipes that are healthy for my body and on the anti-inflammatory list. I am building on my healthy meals and desserts and plan on publishing a recipe book someday.

The wisdom to share with you comes down to this. All diseases are caused by inflammation. Figure out what causes inflammation in your body and you will make your body happy by removing it from your diet. At least cutback. They say the eyes are the window to the soul. The eyes have a way of telling if you are in good or bad health. Your skin, too. It is amazing that when you are eating healthy and putting only good things in your body, your skin reflects these good health choices. If you have dry flaky skin, your skin is telling you something. If you have a rash, your skin is telling you something. The outside of the body often reveals what is going on the inside of our bodies.

Exercise will greatly help reduce and flush out toxins in the body. Sweating is great for the pores! The most difficult thing about exercising is actually not the act of doing it, but the decision to actually do it. For me, that usually means getting my tennis shoes on my feet. Once I get there, it's as good as done. It's the decision, the commitment. I have also learned that when I get my exercise done in the morning, there is a larger chance that it will get done. My schedule gets very busy, and it is easy for me to get caught up and NOT get the work out done in the evening.

The outside of the body often reveals what is going on the inside of our bodies.

I recommend finding something you enjoy doing. It makes it a lot easier to commit. You can also find a workout partner. I have a walking partner. Our goal is to meet each morning, Monday through Friday. Of course, meetings and other commitments may disrupt this, so, it is good to have a backup plan for those days. Either commit to doing your walk anyway or use it as a time to choose an alternative workout. Either way, make the decision, and stick to your commitment to yourself. It is interesting how we are more concerned about letting someone else down and less concerned about letting ourselves down.

We only get one life. One body. One mind. One soul. It is up to us to nurture each of these and commit to taking good care of ourselves. It is no one else's job. I plan to live to at least age 120. The only way I will be successful is to keep and honor my commitment to myself. Whatever your goal is, make it personal and honor yourself. Figure out what is poison to YOUR body and use "food as thy medicine" as your mantra. It can save your life or, at the very least, make it better.

I owe it to my nutritionists, Sarah Bingham and Michelle Trias who helped save my life with their knowledge, patience and commitment to my good health.

Linda's Wisdom Wrap-Up

Healthy eating, smart food choices will make all the difference.

JANELLE HARRIS

FOUNDER / CEO

SHE EXIST MAGAZINE

NEVER FORGET YOUR DREAM

I dedicate my chapter to all the people who have been a victim of bullying in the workplace and leave you with this. Please do not give anyone your power. Your voice is your power and ask God to give you wisdom in order to use your voice. Be your own cheer leader in anything you do.

I was very young when I first began to dream of one day creating a magazine. I would look at all the glossy publications, read the articles, and admire the pictures, all the while thinking to myself that I would one day create something just as beautiful. This dream was something I cherished as I looked at the drab world of the apartment complex that I lived in with my mother.

I became a single parent at the age of eighteen, and I had to deal with postpartum depression and the need to find a job while trying to find someone to watch my son. This put me under such pressure that it threw me into a tailspin from which I almost did not recover. I also had to deal with a stern mother who gave little comfort to me but had plenty of negative advice, telling me, "You made your bed, now lay in it!"

I think the very first piece of wisdom I gained as a mother was to quietly commit to myself that if my son made missteps while he was growing up, I would be there for him to find a solution, not step back and blame him for the outcome. At this point, I could only think this to myself, as I was dependent on family to get me through. I was able to put this piece of wisdom to the test recently when my son got into trouble, and I had to step in to get him back on the right track.

However, as a young mother with no education to speak of, finding a well-paying job seemed impossible. I had to swallow my pride and go into the welfare office and apply for food stamps and other services just to make sure I could feed myself and my baby. I got a bittersweet reprieve from this dark time in my life when my grandmother offered to raise my son, giving me the time I needed to go out and find a job.

I did find an entry-level job, but I knew that getting paid $9 an hour was not the way to create the life of my dreams. And, believe me, I had dreams! I wanted to live somewhere that was green, beautiful, and positive. However, I would then look out my window and reality would set in. But I was determined to change my situation, so I took every opportunity that came my way to learn something new in training classes, also learning from those around me. I was determined to create a life that would eventually get me to my dreams, and I knew I could only do that if I was committed to lifelong learning.

I took every opportunity that came my way to learn something new in training classes, also learning from those around me.

Two years later, while visiting Fredericksburg, Virginia, I discovered a job opportunity for a front desk position that paid $13 an hour. It was in a beautiful building, and I was scared to take the job for fear that I might fail. But I stepped out in faith, took the job, and moved to Virginia. I concentrated on learning how to be better, do better and pay my bills.

When the next job opportunity came along in the same office, it was for $17 an hour and I worked even harder, and I seemed to have found my stride. The owner of the practice was so impressed with my work that he surprised me and promoted me to Office Manager. Now I was on a salary of $45,000 (that was much greater than $17 an hour) and at the age of twenty-two, I was able to purchase my first home. I was coming into my own by applying the wisdom of working hard, staying focused, and continually learning.

It was game on after that, and for the next nine years, I put my heart and soul into my work. I brought in new ideas about marketing and created new processes to streamline the office. I was way ahead of my time in using all the digital tools that were coming out on the market. The owner of the company really appreciated my dedication and hard work and my salary continued to reflect this, until one day the unthinkable happened. My boss had a major accident, and a decision was made to merge with another company.

After the merger took place, I ended up with a new boss, a woman who made it clear from the beginning that she resented having to deal with me. All I can say is she must have felt threatened by me and my stellar reputation. I had naturally created systems that made things easier for other staff members. My new boss, however, questioned every part of every system, almost implying that I was incompetent.

The mental toxicity between me and my new boss continued to rise. She was the master of manipulation. In essence, she seemed to despise me from the very depths of her soul. I was always the last manager to be able to speak at any meeting, and in many cases, she would declare that we were running out of time to block me from speaking. She began to 'forget' to invite me to meetings and even encouraged the other managers to avoid me.

Through all of this, I was still doing my job to the best of my ability. My area of the practice was doing great in the revenue department, and I knew I was an asset to the company. I was totally bemused and puzzled by how a fellow woman could apply such toxic leadership tactics. It got to the point that I went home crying most days, and I began to spiral down into a deep depression that began to trigger physical symptoms that no one could explain.

The only bright spot I could find was when I went home and began to reexamine my dream of one day owning a magazine. I kept playing with ideas, words, and images, knowing that I wanted to create a light for other women to follow, a magazine that would showcase the RIGHT way to be a female leader, and foster a general sense of community among women.

My dream for the magazine began to expand. I realized that I wanted to create something that went far beyond just having people subscribe to a publication. I wanted to create an integrated print, event, and online company that catered to business-minded women by creating a sense of community that was second to none. I wanted to showcase attainable luxury, provide a voice for women to express their dreams, and above all, show everyone what positive female leadership looks like.

However, I first had to deal with my own reality of having a toxic boss and knowing that I could no longer work under such negative conditions. In 2016, I made the decision that I had to leave not only my job but leave Virginia as well. I needed a new environment. I needed more sunshine and I needed to escape the toxicity of my world.

So, after considering two possible job openings, one in California and one in Florida, I decided to head to Tampa, Florida. This was an incredibly hard decision because I also had to decide to leave my son behind. He was established in Virginia, and I did not have the heart to uproot him. So, I made the journey to Tampa solo, knowing that once he finished school he could come and join me.

I wanted to bring individuals, companies, and organizations together to achieve greatness.

I settled into my new job in Tampa, even though it was difficult being the new person, both in the office and in my personal life. I began to meet incredible women, women who had their own dreams and their own businesses, but they could see what I was trying to build and they 'put their shoulders to the wheel' to help me make my dream a reality. I am very grateful to each and every one of them for using their special talents to get us closer to the finish line.

My dream of having a magazine now had a name – **She Exist**. I began to build it digitally online and started to do events to raise money to expand and also raise awareness of my new brand. I wanted to bring individuals, companies, and organizations together to achieve greatness. I began to create workshops and teach new entrepreneurs and businesses the power of unity, collaboration, and branding.

However, issues on the nine to five front meant I needed to move on. I decided to strike out on my own and open a cleaning business, that way I could control my calendar and devote more time to developing the magazine online. When Covid-19 hit in 2020, everyone was thinking that the world was coming to an end, but I saw the opportunity and began to reach out to Hollywood.

The Pandemic was particularly hard on Hollywood, as everyone there is so focused on in-person events and actions. However, I could see the possibilities and I began to reach out and create new opportunities for online collaboration. I was able to give celebrities a digital platform while they were trying to deal with being in a lockdown in the middle of a global pandemic.

One day I decided it was finally time to quit dreaming and to really begin the 'doing' of creating my dream of owning a magazine. I called John, an old friend who is in publication distribution and I point blank asked him if he thought I could do this. He replied it was possible, but I needed to send him a mockup for him to determine if there was a market for it.

I did more than just the mockup! I actually created all the content and did a seventy-page digital magazine. I didn't hear anything from John for two days, then I got an email asking me to call him ASAP! The distributors had gone over the content and were interested in the concept but wanted to see a printed copy. I contacted a local printer, got the digital magazine printed, hopped on a plane to New York, and presented the finished product to John. He was in the middle of a photo shoot, but when he saw the finished magazine, he was very excited.

Fast forward to May of 2022, and the She Exist Magazine Cover Reveal event, featuring Emmy award-winning journalist and actress Cathleen Trigg-Jones, took place at Magazine Cafe in New York City. This event brought out the who's who of the entertainment and fashion industry. We sold out twice at Cafe Magazine due to the popularity of the publication and I am so proud to have it being showcased among many prominent magazines, including Vogue, Essence, Cosmopolitan, Forbes, and People. I was very proud when Cathleen Trigg-Jones said, "The difference between a dreamer and a doer is action. Dare to turn your dreams into reality." This quote went straight to my heart, as I have spent years "doing" in order to bring my dream into reality!

I still have a long way to go for my dream to fully blossom, but I believe that I have what it takes to get the job done because I live and breathe the dream. I understand that no one will want it more than me, believe in it more than me and I know that no one will understand my "why" besides me. My why starts with my heart. My heart shows how much my desire is for my dream to succeed, and I know how much I believe in myself and what I'm doing. It's all about mindset and commitment.

On my way to making my dream a reality, I have gathered other pieces of wisdom. I've learned it is important for you to change the company you keep. You must be around a target audience that is in a different space than you are, one that is successful and positive. Then, you must change your verbiage and speak their language. When I started in my career, I was only eighteen years old, and yet I was able to watch, learn and then eventually teach doctors how to promote themselves. I educated MD's from Johns Hopkins, teaching them how to expand their territories, build their word-of-mouth referrals, grow their client base, and deliver customer service utilizing cutting-edge technology. I was way ahead of my time, all because I was continually learning and applying my newfound knowledge.

I was able to show my trust and love for everyone who has been with me on this journey when we had a major event in Tampa in August of 2022 to show that *She Exit* magazine is well on its way to success. I was able to honor many of the women who have supported me along this journey, and now I am proud that I am able to 'give back' by showcasing them in the magazine. We had all our 'cover ladies' at the event and we were able to let them speak and show their wisdom and commitment.

Everywhere you look, to the right, to the left, and in the rearview mirror, you will see yourself. Stay true to yourself, your vision, your legacy, and do not let the doubters get you down.

Finally, I'd like to leave you with this wisdom. Everywhere you look, to the right, to the left, and in the rearview mirror, you will see yourself. Stay true to yourself, your vision, your legacy, and do not let the doubters get you down. Be the best version of yourself to lay the foundation for a bright future. Life, for me, is a foundation that's built with loyalty, trust, and love. I want to encourage anyone with a dream to not let anyone whisper negative words in your ear or allow anyone to replace where you know you should be. Listen to the voice within you; stay committed to that.

With love and appreciation to Linda Bruns for pushing me in the right mindset to write my chapter.

Linda's Wisdom Wrap-Up

Working under toxic personalities is not healthy for anyone. Women supporting women will lead to healthy relationships!

JOAN HAMMER

IT'S ABOUT FUN

Dedicated to all who are searching for the wisdom inside you. To all I would say look for the wisdom in your lives and follow your heart.

I grew up in the most magical place in the world, New Orleans. The people were wonderful, like a big inclusive family, and there is so much to do, and so many good places to go. Even as a kid, I thought restaurants were great. We had our own waiter at Antoine's, and we knew the chef and sous chef who prepared special meals just for us. I remember a donkey attached to a cart with the driver calling out to come buy produce. I remember the rain falling on one side of the street and sun shining on the other. One year, my mom was the Mardi Gras queen of one of the "crews", also I remember being able to be in the parade. One time I wore the ugliest dress to the ball. I also remember the time there was so much rain during one storm that we put a rowboat in the street instead of our car.

When I was fifteen, life totally changed when my parents divorced. My mom was the best mother anyone could have. She was fun and did crazy stuff like orchestrating taffy pulls across our sizable den.

At one point, we went to Biloxi for a weekend, my two brothers and I, where I remember playing "baseball" with a crumpled-up paper wads. She was an energetic and a very creative mother.

When I was older, we left New Orleans and moved to North Miami where my wonderful grandmother provided us with a wonderful place to live with many comforts. Nothing about my life, as I knew it, really changed other than having lost the plans and dreams of the younger me and having to leave everyone I knew and all of the places I was comfortable in, and the city I loved behind.

Florida was not a great experience for me. I was entering tenth grade as a high schooler and I knew no one, so of course I generally hated it. It is interesting now that this is where I currently live. I did meet my future husband, Glen when we were in high school together. This proved to be a great relationship and next February 2023, we will celebrate our fiftieth wedding anniversary.

After high school, I graduated from a small liberal arts college in Wilkes-Barre, Pennsylvania. I don't know if I learned much but I do remember having a lot of fun. My memories recall that I went out to dinner quite often and those memories have tons of fun times and plenty of laughter, the laughter I ended up depending on to get me through my college years. In fact those four years I felt like I was living under what I termed a "black cloud" which was always present. Unfortunately for me this best describes my experience at Wilkes-Barre.

As I was not a favorite of the Dean of Women, and she wasn't one of my favorites either. I think each semester she secretly hoped I would not come back for the next enrollment. I tried not to let her negative demeanor to me affect my focus. In the end and to her dismay, I did return semester after semester until I graduated, not with honors but nonetheless I completed my courses and got my degree. Thinking back, I believe the best part of my college life was that I enjoyed so much of it during the fun times with friends. After some many years, it was the fun I remember today. There is much wisdom in this type of living in those years of your life.

After college, I was off to where my mother was living in New York. I found a job in the "city" which I loved. It was a small company, and I was their first real employee. I traveled quite a bit, setting up new clients and basically adored my job. The president of the company, an alumnus of Wharton along with my uncle, may have helped me being chosen for the job. As I remember this interview, I also remember we shared a strawberry milkshake. Things were a little bit different in the onboarding process, back then.

Once married, we moved to Florida, and Glen and I opened a business. Our company specialized in extended warranties. As partners, he was the innovator, and I was the implementer. He was great at culvating business and new clients and I was great at everything else. I was leading operations, administration and keeping our company in the right direction, the direction set by my husband. It was definitely a different environment in business for women then. In all my husband and I were a good combination. We made a great leadership team. So great, in fact, that there was an article about us in *Forbes Magazine*.

I also opened our Canadian office in Montreal, a city I very much enjoyed. It was a very good experience. I remember conducting interviews in the bar area of the Ritz Carlton. I would hire all the staff we needed to make this office a success. Montreal ended up being a very profitable office for us. We had all of the Canadian telephone companies as clients. I can tell you I kept in contact with many of that staff from that office as recently as about three years ago.

I remember this interview, I also remember we shared a strawberry milkshake. Things were a little bit different in the onboarding process, back then.

With our successful business and working partnerships, it was both rewarding and profitable. We had many good years for our family and my husband and I.

These days I no longer work and have to say I miss it. The stimulation, thinking, planning, and problem solving. I mainly miss the fun of it all. With my daughter becoming the parent, sometimes I feel that I live more in the shadows than on the main stage. Some of this is what I think what aging is about. In general, I'm adjusting, however aging isn't easy and, as is said, not for the faint of heart. I have learned that we all have to come to grips with getting older and so we should do it as best we can. We go through so many changes and become many different people in our own life along the way. Hopefully, our life journey will move us to grow to be good people and enjoy where we are at the moment, we are experiencing life. I would like to think we can pass what we've learned and lived through as wisdom to others. Our children, people around us, and everyone we touch, I hope I have benefitted them in some way, to me that is a good legacy!

My advice to anyone, and everyone, is to enjoy the adventure that is your life. Build strong family relationships and strong friendships, and while this may not have been something I have been the best at, I believe I have mostly tried to have fun. Don't take yourself so seriously that you lose the sense of yourself or your sense of humor.

Enjoy the adventure that is your life.

Going forward I hope to laugh so much I need lots of Botox for my laugh lines. I hope to still cook and create in the kitchen. I hope to travel so much more than I already have. Today I wish I had known that I should make more notes about the things I cherish so I don't forget them or forget the times I've most treasured the most. This leads me to tell you to keep a diary or journal. Good luck to you as you travel down your own path to create your own adventures.

Now my future is filled with the people in my "new" life. We laugh, we have fun, and we all drink more than some might think we should. But nobody is keeping score because no one can keep track in the midst of our fun. Enjoy more fun in all the stages of your life! Two words…have fun!

I dedicate this to my daughter who walks in light and has so much wisdom.

Linda's Wisdom Wrap-Up

It's all about fun, at the end of the day, it's the experiences we remember, not always the achievement.

HELEN VELLA

THINGS HAPPEN FOR
A REASON

*There is only one of you and you are a unique
original and originals are always better than copies.*

The year is 1995. I'm on a stage in South London, speaking about confidence to an audience of about 150 people, mainly women. I have been studying, coaching, and teaching what I know on this topic of mindset and transformation for years. I'm confident that I know my stuff, and I'm sure that I can impart my knowledge easily with no problem at all.

But I do not *feel* confident about myself or what I am about to do. It's in that moment that I realize having confidence and being confident are definitely two different things. Go figure!

Being confident and feeling confident - that's what I'm here to teach my clients. And it is that intense emotion, that *feeling* of confidence, that makes all the difference. To best achieve a goal, always partner it with a strong, positive emotion. You must *feel* good to *be* good. Positive mantras, when you pair them with matching positive feelings, will be more effective and will last much longer. This has been proven

*You must **feel**
good to **be** good.*

time and time again. Make sure the positive mantras you are using actually make you FEEL positive.

To illustrate this concept, I always give my audience a task, and leave the stage to practice a technique called 'The Circle of Confidence'. In this exercise, you imagine a circle in front of you on the floor, you start to feel the confidence, pride, and positivity well up inside by remembering past experiences where you felt confident, motivated, and so on and then you place yourself -- the self the way you want to be and feel -- in the circle. Then multiply the feeling ten times and stay there for two minutes. When you step outside the circle you take the feelings with you, and you will discover that you have amazing, positive energy.

For me, that was my most confident self, in front of the audience, remembering what I was here for and coming across knowing, looking, feeling, and *being* confident. I did this until the feeling became so intense that I wanted to burst out of myself. I stepped into my visualization, took a deep breath, and I became that person. I walked back onto the stage *feeling* confident, *being* confident, and this made all the difference to my presentation. It also reconfirmed my belief in me to keep practicing what I preach.

Often, I must remind myself to be confident because if like me, you'd been told throughout your childhood that you're no good, or that you will not amount to anything, it's easy to grow up believing this is so. If your successes are not recognized during your childhood years, then your self-esteem and what you think about yourself can be permanently damaged. Until you get help to change your mindset and release the past, you may never think you're good enough. All my life, no matter what successes I've accomplished, in my mind I sometimes still battle the feeling that I'm not good enough. I know most people can relate to this concept.

Many of us get embarrassed if we receive a compliment. Accepting a "well done" is sometimes just difficult. It took me until I was well into my 40s to realize and accept that I was good at what I did, and that others believed I had something to contribute. Until we can recognize our strengths and honor the positive things that make us who we are, we limit our own ability to achieve true success. We also limit ourselves with our relationships, especially intimate relationships.

A few months ago, I was asked to give a presentation to a businesswomen's group on the topic of "Perception of Women in the Workplace". When I arrived, I was somewhat startled to learn that the topic on the agenda had been changed to "The Power of Women in the Workplace."

While I was sure that we had not agreed on that topic, I was confident that I could come up with something good. I was unusually calm about the whole thing, being asked to speak on a topic I had not prepared. "Odd," I thought to myself, but I didn't dwell on this change, as I strongly believe things happen for a reason. I knew I'd be fine.

As I started to mingle with the ladies who were arriving and networking, I heard a few conversations that touched on confidence, perception, families, and juggling the life-work balance. I noticed the mix of women and age groups and felt an energy of acceptance and comfort. None of the women knew I was the guest speaker at this point.

As the event started, I was thinking about what my opening was going to be. I decided I would let things take their course. After my introduction, however, I learned that the topic had changed yet again. Now, I was supposed to speak about "The Power and Perception of Women."

Thankfully, I was feeling good about myself and as I took the stage and began to speak, what came out of my mouth surprised even me! I started talking about how I had lived most of my life trying not to be my mother. Trying to be the opposite of this mother who was physically and emotionally abusive to me and my siblings. My mother kept a sloppy home and unkept children and I nearly always felt unsafe. I grew up feeling fearful trying to be one step ahead of what might happen depending on my mother's mood. Her emotional abuse included always putting me down and telling me I would never amount to anything. She even kept threatening to put me up for adoption. It was a dreadful way to be brought up.

I went on to tell them how I had seen a motivational speaker at a conference I attended who really inspired and motivated me, and I decided there and then that I wanted to be like her. She was so captivating and held 4,000 plus people's attention for the entire length of her presentation.

For years, my motivation was always about trying not to be like my mother in any way, shape, or form, while trying to be like the motivational speaker I so admired. Until the day it hit me that the real question should be, "Who am I? Who is Helen?" I had spent so much of my life trying to be or not be someone else, that I had not focused at all on who I was.

In front of this room full of strangers, I found myself sharing one of my deepest, darkest secrets -- a secret that I hadn't ever spoken of. Not to my family, my friends, or to anyone. It was hard to admit, even to myself. It had to be kept a secret. And the secret was my childhood, the years filled with abuse and neglect.

I had spent so much of my life trying to be or not be someone else, that I had not focused at all on who I was.

I see this pattern of abuse, physical and emotional, repeated when I counsel people of all ages. I know because I have personally lived this. All of it. My father was an alcoholic, my brother attempted suicide twice, and my niece had an eating disorder and died at forty-three because of it. One of my other nieces harmed herself. All my family had therapy and all of them experienced childhood trauma as they perceived it, and their self-abuse of choice was their way of coping.

After the presentation, I felt better about delivering a talk than I had ever felt before. It was amazing. I knew it was time I spoke about my life openly and not keep it inside like a dirty secret anymore. I knew it was the right thing to do, and more importantly, my feelings were reinforced when several women in the group came up to me afterward and said I could have been talking about them because they'd lived very similar lives. Finding this out was an amazing relief and very enlightening.

Again, I got the intense feeling this was the right way to proceed. I was surprised and amazed. I teach every day in some way shape or form, but this was unusual for me to open up and share from my heart. I have always been private about my childhood as I thought our family was the only family that was like this. I now realize that dysfunction, unfortunately, is the norm for many families.

Not sharing your experiences, ideas, feelings, dreams, and goals can make you very ill, both mentally and physically. This also happens in relationships and in business. Sharing your experiences helps you find out how to be more creative and gaining a different perspective on things can make you feel better. We tend to go through life thinking we are the only ones going through what we are going through.

A great exercise I was taught is where you write down some 'reclamation statements'. This is where you write down everything you would like in your life and then change it to a present-day statement as if you already have it. There was a big build-up to the writing down of this information. The facilitator asked if anyone would like to share what they had written. I thought I would volunteer because as a speaker I know how hard it is to get audience participation.

I was reading off my list to the rest of the group when suddenly I burst into tears. One of the things that I had written and not realized was that I had forgiven my mother for what she had done and thanked her for giving me the determination to be who I am today.

Not sharing your experiences, ideas, feelings, dreams, and goals can make you very ill, both mentally and physically.

I do not remember writing it and was shocked when I read it back. It was a turning point in my healing that day. It was also something positive I had been given from my childhood. All these years I had always looked back and could not find many positive aspects of what my mother had given me. What an amazing awakening this was for me. I still have the same determination today.

Again, I believe things happen for a reason. The unconscious mind will take you where you need to be taken, and the powers that be will look after you if you let them. In letting myself just talk, and share from the inside, it became clear that not only was it the right thing for me, but it was also a way that I could make a difference for others.

I have learned a lot of things in my lifetime, and one is when you are down on yourself, and you choose to have low self-esteem this is also how others will see you, and ultimately, treat you. In the past, I would let people take advantage of me. Today, I come from a different place and people treat me differently because I choose how I want to be treated. I am always aware now of my instincts, and I am not afraid to follow them or speak out.

As one of my friends advised me that the best way to deal with such situations is to "bless and release". So, that is what I do - I bless them and release them. I no longer need to take on other people's 'stuff' and try to sort out how they are feeling or try to make them feel better by always thinking it is my fault. Let them go without judging them. Everyone is an individual, and this is what makes the world go round. Help someone who wants to accept help because they have been put in your path for that reason, but if they do not accept your help, simply release them.

Looking back at my difficult start in life, I feel very blessed by what I have been able to achieve and the people that I have been able to help along the way. As I sit here watching the ocean on the balcony of my friend's home in sunny Florida, I reflect on how grateful I am for my friends, my network, and the life I have led up to this point.

My husband recently died, and I find myself alone. I am not lonely, however, as I have these amazing friends and plenty to do, and I try to always volunteer to help and empower my clients. I have been on my own before, so doing things by myself does not faze me at all. I recently went on my first solo cruise and enjoyed every minute of my alone time. I am motivated and looking forward with excitement to the next chapter of my life.

If I could pass some wisdom along to the generations after me, it would be this: Be who you are. Admire people or dislike people, but do not take their behaviors to be yours. Enjoy finding out who you are and be all that YOU are destined to be. Everyone is unique and has their own beauty and wisdom to share if they only seek it out, find it, and share it. It takes work and it was hard for me to open up and accept my past, but it was worth it. You owe it to the world to be who you are, as you are a gift to the world!

Admire people or dislike people, but do not take their behaviors to be yours.

Dedication to my grandchildren Ella and Alia.
Always keep being your own unique self and capture your dreams.

Linda's Wisdom Wrap-Up

What is your "reclamation statement" can you take the time
to discover where it comes from?

MINDY SCARLETT

MANAGING DIRECTOR
SCARLETT CREATIVE GROUP

WHERE'S YOUR PLAN B?

To the young woman contemplating marriage –
make sure you keep your financial identity.

I did not realize when I began writing a marketing term paper on the advertising methods of the Coca-Cola company that I was about to change the entire trajectory of my life. I was a sophomore in college and had just changed my major from architecture to marketing, and I was having great fun doing the research for my paper. However, this was back in the '80s when technology was changing rapidly. I had to graduate from a Remington electric typewriter to a word processor which I had never used, so I headed to the Writing Lab on campus to get some help.

The manager of the writing center was a master's student from Australia. I was intrigued by his accent, and he was very helpful in getting me used to the new technology (which was a state-of-the-art Commodore word processor that used a floppy disk). We became good friends and began to do things other than writing. He made it clear he wanted to be more than friends - I countered with an adamant desire to keep things on the friendship level.

Fast forward seven months, and he finally won the argument. At the grand old age of nineteen, I decided to dive into the matrimonial pool – but with a twist. I was marrying someone who was twelve years older than me, and I was following him back to his hometown of Melbourne, Australia, a place I had never even visited!

I saw this as an adventure, packed up three suitcases and a steamer trunk, and proceeded to drive across the US before catching a Qantas Flight to Melbourne (much to my family's chagrin). This was my first time out of the US, and my inexperience at traveling showed when I misread the tickets by not factoring in the international date line. This meant that my introduction to my in-laws was while they were standing at the airport waiting for us, as we would not arrive until twenty-four hours later.

Here I was, beginning a marriage in a foreign country where my spouse was the only person I knew. I had not completed my college degree, and we were living in a camper van in my in-law's front garden. While this was certainly a case of having the deck stacked against us, I had grown up in a family where the word 'divorce' was not even in the dictionary. When you got married, it was for better or for worse, and it certainly was for life, and I was determined that this was going to be a success.

I was determined to 'make a go' of both my marriage and living in Australia and threw myself into creating a home and a life for both of us. I soon found a job (and so did he) and we were able to move into our own apartment and afford a 1969 white VW beetle as a form of transportation. Luckily this was only needed for weekend trips, as I could get to work on the extensive tramway system in Melbourne.

Being an American in Melbourne actually turned out to be a good thing. My accent made me stand out, and I was able to get good jobs even though I had not finished my degree. Three years after arriving in Australia, I landed a job at the Peter MacCallum Cancer Institute. They were happy to send me back to school, and after moving to a job at National Mutual, I finally graduated with my BA in Public Relations with a minor in business.

While I was climbing the corporate ladder and began to earn some serious money, my husband was still stuck in contract teacher mode. What this meant was he only got paid for nine months of the year. So, I had to take any extra money I earned and put it aside to ensure we could pay bills for the three months every year when he did not bring home a paycheck. It was also up to me to put money aside for major projects, like updates to our home.

Being the absent professor type, my husband would spend these three months reading, studying, and eventually writing, both articles and books. Unfortunately, none of these pursuits made any money. By being very careful with the finances, I was able to bridge the gap, but it also meant that we were not able to save much. We also had the agreement that I would get to go home every year to see my family and that was a hefty investment in plane tickets and holiday money.

Even with all these financial challenges, we finally managed to buy a house in the small town of Woodend, about an hour north of Melbourne. There was an amazing rail system, and I was able to commute back and forth on the train most days. There was a whole quorum of people who lived in the small towns around Woodend, and soon we formed a social club of sorts.

While different people would take different trains on weekdays, on Friday almost everyone would take the 5:11 train on the Bendigo line. We became known as the 5:11 social club. We would all bring a little something to eat and drink, and we would have almost an hour to chat, catch up and even plan other social events in places other than the first train car.

By the time we hit our ten-year wedding anniversary, my husband was still just a contract teacher. I began to be a bit concerned and decided it was time to start planning for retirement. I opened a 401K account and began to make plans for other investments.

In the meantime, my husband was working on a book based on the history of the Windsor Hotel, a grand European-style hotel in downtown Melbourne. I very much wanted to help him with it, but he was too egotistical to listen to any of my suggestions, so in the interest of peace I left him to his long stints of research, either at the library or in his study in our home.

I turned to other pursuits, going to stained glass workshops and making beautiful things for our home, and slowly remodeling every room in our house. We had since moved to a larger home on the outskirts of Woodend and we had five acres of beautiful gardens with amazing outbuildings. Everyone from the 5:11 social club would come for BBQs, and I threw major birthday parties for my best friend who had six children, and they kept turning eighteen and they needed to have a place to throw their parties!

Careerwise I had been climbing the corporate ladder, but the onset of corporate burnout made me decide to step out on my own and I began my own public relations company. I was quite proud that the company I had just resigned from became a client and I began adding others. One of my clients was a friend who owned a local winery and was also interested in alternative medicine. This was when I got my first experience as a book ghostwriter.

However, my husband seemed to be going deeper and deeper into absent-minded professor mode. I was the one going out on weekends while he stayed behind on his newly acquired computer, researching and writing. His book on the Windsor Hotel was finally published. It was a lovely, hardcover book and when I turned the pages and read nearly three pages of acknowledgments, my heart stopped. He had thanked everyone in his life, everyone except me! Nowhere was there even a mention that he was married. I was hurt, I was appalled, and it was a wake-up call!

I was hurt, I was appalled, and it was a wake-up call!

Shortly after that, I found a cartoon that showed a woman carrying an anniversary cake that had three layers. The bottom layer said, "First five years of marriage great," the second tier said, "The next five years so-so" and the final tier said, "Last few months, really bad." I showed my husband this cartoon and said that this was how I was feeling, and I thought that we should see someone to help get our relationship back on track.

His response to this was to say he felt it was too late to do anything about our relationship, and he had already made plans to return to the US to begin work on his next book. When he returned, he was going to live in a different town. My heart stopped and I was speechless. His further expectation was that I would continue to live at the house, of course this meant that I would be paying the mortgage, while he was dashing around writing books and looking for other places to live.

I was leaving the next day on a business trip to Sydney. I had a client who was launching a book, and I had an entire weekend of media coverage to handle and a book launch to execute. Thankfully, I was able to keep my composure together and the press loved the new book. Like a robot, I kept putting one foot in front of the other, with a fixed smile plastered on my face, not at all sure of what I was going to do when I got back home. I could not believe that I was dealing with divorce – a word that did not exist in my family's dictionary.

I arrived back at the house in Woodend, and after a few nights of sleeping on the sofa, I rented an apartment and moved out of the house. I kept my head down and worked night and day for the Work and Family Life Agency which was my main client. When they decided to make the position I was covering permanent, I applied. However, someone with more experience in book sales 'scooped' the pool and I was passed over. This was the last straw, and I decided that it was time to return to the US where my family would be ready, willing, and able to support me both financially and emotionally. I had not seen this marriage breakup coming and it had definitely knocked all the apples off of my apple cart. So, I packed up my original three suitcases, liquidated my 401K to buy a plane ticket, and headed back to the good ole' USA.

I could not believe that I was 30 years old and starting over in every sense of the word. I had lost everything, my home, my business, my circle of friends. I was in what felt like a foreign country, (even though I had been born here) trying to figure out how to survive and rebuild a life when all I could do was go from crying jag to crying jag. One of my biggest fears was how my parents were going to react to my marriage breakdown. However, their stance was it was not my fault and that I should just get on with my life. They were there to support me in any way I needed.

In my mind, I was returning home, to the country where I had grown up. However, the reality was much different! Everyone had an accent, I was handling green money again (Australian money is very colorful, almost as if it comes from a Monopoly game) and I found that I was at an extreme disadvantage as I had no work history in the US to speak of, and I had no credit rating.

The bottom line was that I did not exist as an adult in the US. I had never applied for a credit card, owned a car, or done any of the other things that people do to create a credit profile. Could I have done these things on my visits back home? Yes, I could have, but it never entered my mind that I would end up divorced and on my own!

I had never planned for what I would do in this situation because remember, in my family, divorce was not in the dictionary.

I was lucky that I had a supportive family. My brother was a car dealer and he handed me the keys to a loaner car and told me to keep it for as long as I needed to. I couch-surfed between my parents' house and my brother's house while I looked for work, but freelance and contract work seemed to be the only options for a person with no American work history. The first work I found was as a freelance writer for the South Bend Tribune and the South Bend Executive Journal. The only problem was, I did not own a computer. Luckily, I had a friend from college who offered me the use of her computer so I could at least earn some money. I also discovered the hard way that it is better to have a bad credit rating than no credit rating.

I will be forever grateful to the female bank manager who finally took pity on me, and gave me a loan for $500 to buy a computer so that I could do my freelance writing and I could also begin work on my credit rating. Soon after that, I was able to get a car loan and move to Chicago where I rented my own apartment. This accomplishment had taken me two years to achieve, and because I was still working freelance, my income was still not stable, so it wasn't easy.

All of the major changes in my life seem to ride on the heels of changes in technology. When I finally was ready to begin dating, there was something new on the horizon called the Internet, and there was then something called AOL Personals, so I decided to post my details. I soon heard from someone named David who was a stockbroker in New York. At first, I was dismissive, as I found him to be geographically challenged - he was in Manhattan, and I was in Chicago, so what was the point?

We finally graduated to the phone, where our first conversation lasted for five hours, and for the next five weeks, we were glued to opposite ends of the same phone line. We spent hours and hours talking about our hopes and dreams, and his dream was to get married and start a family. After several years of dating commitment-phobic guys, this was a welcome change. All of these deep conversations then led to the inevitable question, how could we connect in person? His response was to send me a ticket to New York. Three hours after I landed, David proposed, and I spent the entire weekend coming up with reasons why that would not work.

The decision point came on Sunday, when David held up my return ticket and said we had to order a cab to get to the airport on time if I was going to use it. I remember a very long moment, when I could see two very different roads in front of me, one where I stayed and got married, and one where I left and went back to Chicago. The road to matrimony won out, and a week later we got married in City Hall in Manhattan, with our daughter Shannon making an arrival one day shy of our first anniversary.

I could see two very different roads in front of me.

While we have had an interesting life with both of us as entrepreneurs, I have learned my lesson about financial planning. We now have a retirement fund, I have my own credit rating, and we both have life insurance policies. After twenty-three very happy years, I am confident that I will not have to deal with another divorce, but I still have to deal with the fact that life is unpredictable, and I have to deal with the concept. More importantly I have to plan for it. The bottom line is this – as women, we MUST make plans for our own future. You never know what life will throw at you and you need to be prepared. As women, we need to make sure that we take care of our own financial future. Work on your plan A, but always have a plan B!

This chapter is dedicated to all the people who have helped me along my way, through all the ups and down, with a special thank you to my husband, my daughter and my family.

Linda's Wisdom Wrap-Up

Life is always changing, at minimum we should have a Plan A and a Plan B and maybe a few more waiting in the wings.

LIZA MARIE GARCIA

CHIEF OPERATING OFFICER, NOW PUBLISHING
PRESIDENT CBF TAMPA BAY

RESPECT DEMONSTRATED WISDOM

Listen to the wisdom of those who have traveled before you as sometimes there is no match for the wisdom of experience!

I don't know why I'm struggling so much with writing this chapter. It could be the usual subjects, work, my daughters, the non-profit organization…and on and on, but I don't think it is that easy.

Now as I sit here determined to finish this chapter, I can count restarting it no less than four times. Ironically, living in the publishing world as I do, we don't really believe in *writers block*. In fact we "author coach" our clients in why *writers block* really doesn't exist. Our team, specifically our editors, teach our clients ways to push through it and yet here I sit, writing and re-writing this chapter for one of our very own books.

The wisdom I want to share, though, is the importance of being mentored, as well as becoming a mentor yourself to pay it forward.

At my very first "real job" as a young IBM engineer straight out of college, I had a manager named Kathy Dunn. She had a major impact on my life. So much so that I used her name as my answer for those "security" questions you sometimes have to set up for online accounts. She was my first mentor, and I will always be grateful for her wisdom.

*Why **writers block** really doesn't exist.*

I know it was more than a blessing that my first management experience was not only with a female direct report, but that her management style proved to be such a positive model for me. I've met many women who share with me that they never worked for a great female boss, and in this essay you will learn that I had two significant impactful female managers.

For Kathy Dunn, what I learned was simple yet important. Kathy was the type of person that commandeered respect by simply entering the room. I remember more than a few times being invited to the office conference room, and as Kathy would step in, there was a heightened sense of respect in the air. This is difficult to describe even now. Difficult to put my arms around exactly what the feeling was surrounding her, but I definitely recall the impact. Her title as I remember was the Administration/Operations Manager so she directed most activities in our software branch in Salt Lake City.

I remember Kathy's place in the conference table, full of male management types except for one other female manager, would mostly be in the middle of the room. This would be the days before "Lean In" (book by Sheryl Sandberg) was published. Yes, Kathy did *lean in*, and she did so in a professional and authoritative manner. You would not describe Kathy as aggressive, loud or struggling to make a point or show her prowess. No, when Kathy spoke, all listened. In fact, while Kathy would express her view or opinion the rest of the room made sure they understood and practiced active listening to ensure they didn't miss what she had to say. Kathy was respected because of her demonstrated wisdom and calm and knowledgeable demeanor, no matter the situation. She was an excellent model for me. At the time, my behavior tended to lean opposite of hers, and so being able to observe this woman lead with a gentle stick was a blessing.

About three years later, I was working for Siemens AG after IBM was bought out, and I found myself being led by a project manager named Robyn Button. She had a military background and more degrees than most could count. Robyn was well accomplished and ahead of her time in many respects.

She became my direct report manager, and would eventually be my first client when I left IBM/Siemens to start my first company at twenty-six.

What Robyn taught me was one of the most important lessons a young person can learn at the start of his or her career. Never make decisions when your emotions are running high. This seems simple, yet when you are a young and high-energy person, it is far from easy. I remember vividly her words of wisdom, as well as the "exercise" of sorts that she forced on me.

Robyn's help came at a critical point in my business life. I had taken on a project from my "first" customer, and was contracted to configure software, train employees, and implement a new telecommunications system for the Bon Marche retail brand in sixty stores across the Western United States. This included programming call centers, which were fairly new at the time.

I was a young engineer with a ton of responsibility as I tried to make my way with the "big people" on this account. My office was headquartered in downtown Seattle, behind the retail outlet owned by Macy's. The details are blurry, but I remember having a conflict with a junior engineer working for Macy's, who was not much older than I was. I remember, without a doubt, that I was right and he was wrong (of course). The conflict, however, was bad for the team. I wanted to charge headfirst into the conflict and fix things how I saw fit, but I paused and recognized it was not my responsibility. I had no authority in the situation. It was Robyn who stepped into settle things.

Never make decisions when your emotions are running high.

Robyn took me aside and said, "Never act when emotions are involved." She explained that even good emotions should have no influence over our decisions. She advised that I would regret making decisions fueled by my emotions.

Robyn's demeanor was very similar to Kathy's—calm and collected. Her presence and intelligence were well respected by others, and I can only assume this idea of "keeping emotions in check" contributed to that.

She asked me to do the following: take the elevator to the parking garage, get in my car, and drive around the city block until my emotions calmed and I was back to center. I use "back to center" because that is where I like to be in my life even today.

Robyn gave me this powerful exercise to help me train my behaviors. This was a powerful lesson.

These are just two examples of wisdom-filled, beautiful women mentors I've been blessed to have worked with, along my career path. I have also been a mentor, as I understand the importance of lifting other women up. I am acutely aware that I am my teenage daughters' greatest mentor. I challenge each of you to pay it forward and share the wisdom you have lived through. There is no greater command than to love God our father and take care of his sheep. Mentor the sheep!

For the beautiful souls within the young ladies my daughters are becoming. May you find guidance to show you the open doors you need to walk through and learn never to re-open a door you weren't meant to even knock on.

Linda's Wisdom Wrap-Up

Being reactive is risky, being proactive is effective.

BARBARA A. GLANZ

CSP, CPAE

HALL OF FAME SPEAKER

WHAT DO YOU SAY TO YOUR TWENTY YEAR OLD SELF?

May you be inspired to learn from your experiences, especially the difficult ones, and to find the good in every situation. That will enable you to have more love for others, including yourself, and to find ways to make a difference every single day.

A s the author of fourteen books and a professional speaker who has traveled the world, I have never been asked the question, "What wisdom would you give your twenty-year-old self?"

I think I was pretty mature at age twenty, perhaps due to being the oldest of four children and growing up in a small town. Thinking back, I believe I made very good decisions growing up, such as choosing to spend a lot of time practicing the piano, doing my best in school, and choosing where to go to college.

Whatever I focused on, I always did to the very best of my ability, a lesson I learned as a very young person. This led to many awards and honors. I also made an excellent choice in a husband, falling in love with the most honest and loyal person I have ever known...and he was handsome, too! We raised three beautiful children along the way.

I think one of the important lessons I learned early in life was the idea, "Bloom where you are planted." Find the good in every situation and make the most of it. Some of the wisdom I have gained over the years I think I intuitively knew in those days.

Here are my "bullets of wisdom"!

Bullet #1

Take care of yourself. Eat right, do some exercise every day, find alone time each day, get a good night's sleep, and treasure friends and family. Even in my seventies, I am committed to at least thirty minutes of exercise every day. I either swim a mile, walk three miles on the beach, go to my trainer, or walk on the treadmill. I am so serious about this that even if it is 10:00 pm and I haven't yet exercised, I am on the treadmill in my extra bedroom. Commitment is the key!

You need quiet time each day to refill your emotional bank account and to keep connected to your spiritual self. This can be done through meditation, prayer, journaling, or reading a spiritual book such as a devotional or the Bible.

Bullet #2

Every day is a GIFT. Look for the blessings even in the most difficult situations in your life. If you truly look, you WILL find them. I love the quote from William Winter, "As much of Heaven is visible as we have eyes to see."

When our second child died, it was the hardest thing I ever had to face in my life. However, many blessings came out of that time, and one of them was learning to live five minutes at a time. On the most difficult days when I didn't think I could get out of bed or even get through an hour, I could always make it through five minutes. Just five minutes, and then the next five minutes.

What that taught me was to always be fully in the present. When I am with someone, I am totally with them. This is what mindfulness is about. "Every day is a gift. That is why we call it 'the present.'"

Bullet #3

Nurture your FAITH, whatever that may be for you. It is the only thing that can NEVER be taken away from you. I have learned in my spiritual life that in surrender comes perfect freedom. I just have to trust that no matter how bad things get, God IS in charge. His plan is much better for me than my own plans, and that surrender takes the anxiety of the future away. I must admit, however, that as a human being, I do take control back more often than I should, but I am learning each day to give it up to God.

When I started my company at fifty-two, I said, "God, *You* gave me this gift, so You put me where You want me to be." The result has been the unbelievable opportunity to speak to audiences all over the world. Because I knew from the beginning that I was just the "messenger," I have never gotten caught up in ego (Edging God Out), and my business has all been word of mouth and referral.

I have a new friend who was imprisoned in solitary confinement in Syria for sixty-three days several years ago. He said they took everything from him - his passport, his cell phone, all his contact information, and even his clothes. It was completely dark, and he didn't even know what day it was (though he figured out a system to once a day determine light or dark to try to keep count.) He shares that the ONLY thing they could not take from him was his faith, and that kept him sane through the whole horrible ordeal.

Bullet #4

RELATIONSHIPS are what life is all about. Be the best family member, spouse, parent, and friend you can be with the skills you have been given. And remember, you have to be a friend to gain a friend.

Everything can be taken from us so quickly – our health, our homes, our possessions, the people we love, and yet our relationships and our memories can never be taken away. However, we must make the relationships in our lives a priority, or they can fade away as well.

During the pandemic I decided to do a "100 Day Project." Every day I called one or two people who had influenced my life in some way, many of whom I had not spoken with in years. What a precious gift that was to me – and I hope for them, too! It rekindled many friendships that had gotten buried in busyness.

I keep a "Blessings Journal," and most days I write about the people I interacted with and what blessings I received that day. Sometimes I note the big things, but mostly they are small things that happened in my day, from a phone call, to an email, or a surprise gift. No matter how busy or difficult a day is, I can always find one or two blessings, and most of them come from the relationships in my life.

Also, every Thanksgiving I make a list of all the people in this world that I love. I am always so touched by how long that list has grown to be, and how blessed I am to have so many beautiful relationships.

"Friendship is born at that moment when one person says to another, 'What! You, too? I thought I was the only one.'" ~ C.S. Lewis

Bullet #5

LOVE all people. Even if you do not agree with them or don't even like them, they were still created in the image of God, so RESPECT them as human beings. Keep in mind that does not mean that you must spend time with them!

I believe that our only responsibility in life is simply to love other people as we meet them on our journey. I often tell this story about an experience I had in the ladies restroom at O'Hare airport as a simple example. It was a cold, snowy February morning, and as I walked into the restroom, there was a woman all hunched over, listlessly cleaning, simply going through the motions. I walked up to her, lightly touched her on the arm, looked right into her eyes, and said, "Thank you so much for keeping this restroom clean. You are really making a difference for all of us who travel."

I believe that our only responsibility in life is simply to love other people as we meet them on our journey.

She looked at me like a doe in the headlights and then out came a big smile. She perked up, and she started cleaning with a passion. By the time I came out of the stall, she was handing out towels to all the women who were washing their hands. I left with tears in my eyes because that cost me nothing. My words to her, a sentence only, told her she was of value, and I saw her as a human being with a purpose.

After hearing that story, my audience members tell me they never go into a restroom where someone is cleaning without thanking them. That is just one simple example of how choosing to make human level connections can make such a difference in this world. My personal philosophy of life has come from Mother Teresa: "Be kind and merciful. Let no one ever come to you without coming away better and happier."

Bullet #6

Learn to FORGIVE, not for the other person (they probably will never know), but for yourself. Holding grudges eats away at you, so forgive and let go. That goes for yourself as well! We are only human, and we ALL make mistakes. So, let us forgive others for their mistakes.

I suggest that my audiences think about "mis-takes." Even in the movies, it takes many takes to get a final scene, so a "mis-take" is just one thing that didn't work.

"The person who succeeds is not the one who holds back, fearing failure, nor the one who never fails…but rather the one who moves on in spite of failure." ~ Charles Swindoll

Bullet #7

Read and LEARN something new every day. This keeps you growing and young, even if you are chronologically older. I have been a reader my entire life. One of my favorite quotes is from S. I. Hayakawa: "In a very real sense, people who have read good literature have lived more than people who cannot or will not read. It is not true that we have only one life to live: if we can read, we can live as many more lives and as many kinds of lives as we wish." I suggest you keep a list of all the books you read every year. It is so affirming to go back and realize all the experiences you have had through your reading.

It is so important, too, for us to be open to learning new things, especially with technology today. I am so proud of my ninety-eight-year-old aunt who uses email every day and even knows how to Zoom to connect with one of her sons in Thailand. When the pandemic started, I had to learn how to present on Zoom, how to do webinars for my clients, and how to scan documents rather than faxing them. Although you might have said I had to be hauled into all this technology kicking and screaming (as I am not a techy person), I have continued to learn because I know that in the twenty-first century, technology is here to stay.

One example was being asked to do a Zoom keynote speaker event to over 3000 people. I don't think I slept well for a week, worrying if the technology would fail. It went well, but I still missed the personal interaction. However, I learned from this event. Continual learning keeps our minds sharp as well as open to new ideas, and of course, it means we can keep up with technology.

Bullet #8

Be RESILIENT. No matter what happens in your life, you always have choices in how you respond. I appreciate this quote from Florence Littauer: "I am not responsible for my situation, but I am responsible for my reaction to it."

Like so many others in their later years, I have had a lot of pain in my life. We lost our second child, Gavin, when I was just twenty-eight years old, and it was the hardest thing I will ever have to bear. In that same year, my dad died unexpectedly at age sixty-two, our St, Bernard puppy died, and I found a lump in my breast. Finally, my dear husband Charlie died when I was just fifty-six. I was very young to be a widow, so it was an extremely lonely time for me. However, I learned that I could either be better or bitter – it was my **CHOICE**.

Bullet #9

Find your TRIBE. It helps so much to have some kind of support group around you to help you see the bigger picture. Professionally, I am in a Mastermind group of speaker friends from all over the country. We meet once a month and share ideas and challenges. Personally, I am in a sharing group from my church as well as a Bible study that meets weekly. I also created a book group of friends that keep me grounded and help expand my horizons. There are many resources on the internet today that can help you find a place where you feel you are not alone and you can share your concerns safely. That will help you keep difficult times in perspective.

Follow your dreams and dream BIG. Growing up in a town of 4,500 in Iowa in the 50s and 60s, my dreams were limited by my experience and the people I knew. As I went off to college and experienced a bigger world, however, my dreams became bigger and bigger. I realized early on in my life that I could be and do anything I set my mind to, and I am grateful to my parents for that teaching. I learned to "always aim for the top."

Finally, remember that you CAN have it all. I was a high school English and Drama teacher for several years before our children were born. In fact, one of the fun things I share in the introduction to my audiences is that I directed David Hasselhoff in his first high school play! When our first child was born, Charlie and I decided that I would stay home and make them my career. I had a business plan and goals for them. By age seven they had all seen a ballet, an opera, and a stage play, and I took them to classes at all the museums in downtown Chicago. In addition to these culture-filled outings, they had to take piano lessons from their seventh birthday to their twelfth birthday, and this was non-negotiable.

During the nineteen years I stayed at home with them, I did some part-time teaching, and I finished my Master's Degree in Adult Learning, one course a quarter for five years. Then at age forty-eight, when our oldest son was going off to Dartmouth, I went back to work as Manager of Training for a Times Mirror Company. At age fifty-two I started my own company as a professional speaker and author, and the rest has been amazing.

Even in my wildest dreams I never imagined I could accomplish and experience all the blessings I have in my life, mostly after the age of fifty. I've been inducted into the Speaker Hall of Fame, I am the first speaker on record to speak in all fifty states and on all seven continents, and I have been blessed to visit over 100 different countries. If a small-town girl from Iowa can do all that, so can you!

The message my parents taught me was to believe in myself and to always do my best. That is enough! And I believe that when we do that, doors open that we could never have imagined. So, never give up on yourself or your dreams. You CAN have it all!

These words are dedicated to my God who has never left me even when I may have momentarily left Him in times of overwhelming personal pain and to my dear children and grandchildren on earth and my precious husband and son in Heaven.

Linda's Wisdom Wrap-Up

Truly each day is a gift. A key could be taking it 5 minutes at a time.

AUTHOR'S FINAL WISDOM

I know I'll never know it all
There is a process in learning
I learn through the process
I always do everything right unless I'm not
I learn even when I don't do something right so, it isn't a total waste of time or experience
Remember, it's a process
Creative thinking is empowering
Empowerment is empowering
Loyalty can burn you sometimes
Loyalty is still the best way
I have to be loyal to myself before I can expect to be loyal to others and others to me
Two wrongs still don't make a right
Doing the right thing is still right
Faith is faith, without it you have worry
You can't have faith and worry at the same time
It is my option which I choose
Smart work is more valuable than hard work
When your chips are down, you can count on your true friends
When my chips are up, I make sure my friends can count on me
When a friend is crying for help, sometimes it comes out in evil ways
Either way, it is still a cry for help
Success is measured by…you fill in the blank
It is different for everyone
Don't let others define your success
You are the only one who can decide what that means to you
*You do **you** if it's not hurting you or anyone around you*

What I've learned in recent years

I can depend on my self
I can ask for help
I can depend on other people
Love is all around
I set my own limitations

My life motto

Think, say, and act with love in your heart and you can't go wrong!

Acknowledging the Contributors

Currently, what I am tremendously grateful for is each one of the contributing authors for this book, **Wisdom Before Me**. Each have been completely transparent and their gained and shared wisdom is truly impactful. We have contributors with ages spanning five decades. They come from varied backgrounds. Some have been through multiple tragedies and others have been through minor setbacks. Each have gained authentic wisdom that can help someone who may be going through a similar circumstance. As women, we all win when we lift each other up in loving support. We are all in this together. This world is a better place when we work together toward a common goal. We can create a better life and a better world. I could not be more grateful for all their contributions. This is a first-class group of women, and I am honored to have each as a part of this book!

ABOUT THE CONTRIBUTING AUTHORS

LAUREN BILLINGS

Determination

LEGACY MOVING SERVICES

For The Best Moving Experience
By Professional, Experienced Movers

LINDA BRUNS

Courage

Women have needs, too! ™

by *Linda*

WOMEN HAVE NEEDS, TOO!

Inspiring and Empowering Women

ERIN FELDMAN

Perspicacity

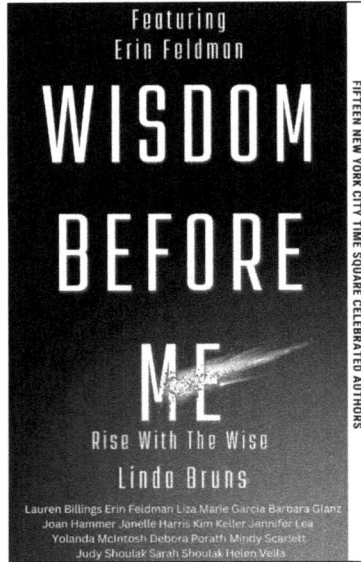

LIZA MARIE GARCIA

Coachability

N◉W
SC PRESS
PUBLISHING

NOW SC Press Publishing

---

*Our Mission is to Publish
the Voice of Purpose*

JOAN HAMMER

JANELLE HARRIS

Wisdom

BARBARA A. GLANZ

Abundance

Barbara Glanz, CSP,CPAE
speaker·author·consultant

"Spreading Contagious Enthusiasm™"

KIM KELLER

Goal Setter

Goals lead to freedom

Trust

ENTRY ENVY

Let Your Front Door Say So Much More

YOLANDA MCINTOSH

Faith

MizMacMarketing LLC

MizMacMarketing LLC

We are waiting for you to help you restart, grow or stabilize your business. We are client focused.

DEBORA PORATH

Jump

Woman of Destiny

Psalm 92:12

Building futures for your independence

MARY KAY

Jump into Your Destiny

MINDY SCARLETT

Planning

The Scarlett Creative Group
Publishing ♦ Ghostwriting ♦ Branding

THE SCARLET CREATIVE GROUP

Self-Publishing, Ghostwriting and Branding

JUDY SHOULAK

Grateful

RELATIVELY SPEAKING

Helping People Become Their Best Selves

SARAH SHOULAK

Discipline

CURRY FORD WEST

Family, Unity, and Legacy

HELEN VELLA

Authentic

VELLA MINDSET STRATEGIES

Mindset is the Key to Transformation

ABOUT THE AUTHOR

Linda Bruns is founder and Chief Inspirer of Women Have Needs, Too!, a company designed to inspire and empower women to live their fullest lives. Throughout her life, she has been dedicated to empowering women, guiding, consulting and inspiring them to live their happiest life. Linda's mission is to remind each woman they are a WINNER! You can watch her in her current online telecast *WomenHaveNeeds, Too!* at WomenHaveNeedsToo.com/WHNTTV where she showcases dynamic women who also inspire and empower women in the areas of health, wealth and mindset.

You can also find Linda on the sidelines coaching women in *The Mission Accelerator*, her one-on-one coaching program designed to help women focus on their mission by growing past their fears, gaining clarity and learning the art of communication with themselves and others. Linda has also been featured as an author in the book *The Top 25 ChangeMakers in Florida*. She is devoted to her family, husband and friends.

Wisdom Before Me is her debut book, however she has many books in her!

www.ingramcontent.com/pod-product-compliance
Lightning Source LLC
Chambersburg PA
CBHW071649210326
41597CB00017B/2162